Unparalleled
Modern Cables Collection
by Knit Picks

Copyright 2023 © Knit Picks

All rights reserved. This book or any portion thereof may not be reproduced or used in any manner whatsoever without the express written permission of the publisher except for the use of brief quotations in a book review.

Photography by John Cranford
Graphic Design by Lee Meredith
Content Direction by Stacey Winklepleck
Creative Direction by Hillary Elliott

Printed in the United States of America
First Printing, 2023

ISBN 978-1-62767-344-0

Versa Press, Inc.

800-447-7829
www.versapress.com

CONTENTS

Ventisca Slipover *by Kristen Jancuk*   **8**

Primrose Pullover *by Megan Gonzalez*   **16**

Flying Trapeze Shawl *by Holli Yeoh*   **26**

Ballinora Cardigan *by Helen Metcalfe*   **34**

Crossings Scarf *by Mone Dräger*   **44**

Scandic Pullover *by Donna Estin*   **50**

Lyan Hat *by Sierra Morningstar*   **58**

Esker Wrap *by Neisha Abdulla*   **64**

Focus Puller Cardigan *by Holli Yeoh*   **70**

Knots Shawl *by Mone Dräger*   **86**

Bricksy Joy Sweater *by Griselda Zárate*   **94**

Pinball Vest *by Sandi Rosner*   **104**

Varja Sweater *by Claire Slade*   **112**

Balter Hat *by Sierra Morningstar*   **122**

Glossary   **124**

VENTISCA SLIPOVER
by Kristen Jancuk

FINISHED MEASUREMENTS
34 (37.5, 42, 45.5, 50)(54.5, 57.5, 62, 65.5, 70)" finished chest circumference; meant to be worn with 4-6" positive ease
Sample is 37.5"; model is 34.5"

YARN
Twill™ (worsted weight, 100 % Superwash Merino Wool; 149 yards/100g): Rose Water Heather 28537, 5 (6, 6, 7, 7)(8, 9, 9, 10, 11) hanks

NEEDLES
US 8 (5mm) 16 and 24" circular needles, or size to obtain gauge

US 7 (4.5mm) 16 and 24" circular needles, or one smaller than size used to obtain gauge

NOTIONS
Yarn Needle
Stitch Markers
Cable Needle
Stitch Holders or Scrap Yarn

GAUGE
24 sts and 30 row = 4" in 1/2 Cable Cross Pattern worked flat, blocked
1 repeat of Chart A, 22 sts x 45 rows = 4" wide and 6" tall

For pattern support, contact mediaperuana@gmail.com

Ventisca Slipover

Notes:
Ventisca is a cozy cabled piece specifically designed for layering! A split hem and long armholes make it easy to slip on over blouses, dresses, or even lighter knits.

Ventisca is worked flat in pieces and seamed, making it easy to customize the length of the side vents.

Charts are worked flat; read RS rows (odd numbers) from right to left, and WS rows (even numbers) from left to right.

2/2 RC (2 over 2 Right Cable)
Sl2 to CN, hold in back; K2, K2 from CN.

2/2 LC (2 over 2 Left Cable)
Sl2 to CN, hold in front; K2, K2 from CN.

2/2 RPC (2 over 2 Right Cable, Purl back)
Sl2 to CN, hold in back; K2, P2 from CN.

2/2 LPC (2 over 2 Left Cable, Purl back)
Sl2 to CN, hold in front; P2, K2 from CN.

1/2 RC (1 over 2 Right Cable)
Sl2 to CN, hold in back; K1, K2 from CN.

1/2 LC (1 over 2 Left Cable)
Sl1 to CN, hold in front; K2, K1 from CN.

1/2 Cable Cross Pattern (flat over a multiple of 7 sts)
Row 1 (RS): (P1, 1/2 RC, 1/2 LC) to end.
Row 2 (WS): (P6, K1) to end.
Rep Rows 1-2 for pattern.

Twisted Rib (flat over an even number of sts)
Row 1 (RS): (K1 TBL, P1) to end.
Row 2 (WS): (K1, P1 TBL) to end.
Rep Rows 1-2 for pattern.

Twisted Rib (in the round over an even number of sts)
Rnd 1: (K1 TBL, P1) to end.
Rep Rnd 1 for pattern.

Chart A (flat over 22 sts)
Row 1 (RS): P1, K2, P2, K4, P4, K4, P2, K2, P1.
Row 2 (WS): K1, P2, K2, P4, K4, P4, K2, P2, K1.
Row 3: P1, K2, P2, 2/2 RC, P4, 2/2 LC, P2, K2, P1.
Row 4: K1, P2, K2, P4, K4, P4, K2, P2, K1.
Row 5: P1, 2/2 LC, K4, P4, K4, 2/2 RC, P1.
Row 6: K1, P8, K4, P8, K1.
Row 7: P1, K2, 2/2 LC, K2, P4, K2, 2/2 RC, K2, P1.
Row 8: K1, P8, K4, P8, K1.
Row 9: P1, K4, 2/2 LC, P4, 2/2 RC, K4, P1.
Row 10: K1, P8, K4, P8, K1.
Row 11: P1, 2/2 LC, K2, 2/2 LC, 2/2 RC, K2, 2/2 RC, P1.
Row 12: K1, P20, K1.
Row 13: P1, K2, 2/2 LC, K8, 2/2 RC, K2, P1.
Row 14: K1, P20, K1.
Row 15: P1, K4, 2/2 LC, K4, 2/2 RC, K4, P1.
Row 16: K1, P20, K1.
Row 17: P1, 2/2 LPC, K2, 2/2 LC, 2/2 RC, K2, 2/2 RPC, P1.
Row 18: K3, P16, K3.
Row 19: P3, 2/2 LC, K8, 2/2 RC, P3.
Row 20: K3, P16, K3.
Row 21: P3, K2, 2/2 LC, K4, 2/2 RC, K2, P3.
Row 22: K3, P16, K3.
Row 23: P3, K4, 2/2 LPC, 2/2 RPC, K4, P3.
Row 24: K3, P4, K2, P4, K2, P4, K3.
Row 25: P3, 2/2 LC, P2, K4, P2, 2/2 RC, P3.
Row 26: K3, P4, K2, P4, K2, P4, K3.
Row 27: P3, K4, 2/2 RC, 2/2 LC, K4, P3.
Row 28: K3, P16, K3.
Row 29: P3, K2, 2/2 RC, K4, 2/2 LC, K2, P3.
Row 30: K3, P16, K3.
Row 31: P3, 2/2 RC, K8, 2/2 LC, P3.
Row 32: K3, P16, K3.
Row 33: P1, 2/2 RC, K2, 2/2 RC, 2/2 LC, K2, 2/2 LC, P1.
Row 34: K1, P20, K1.
Row 35: P1, K4, 2/2 RC, K4, 2/2 LC, K4, P1.
Row 36: K1, P20, K1.
Row 37: P1, K2, 2/2 RC, K8, 2/2 LC, K2, P1.
Row 38: K1, P20, K1.
Row 39: P1, 2/2 RC, K2, 2/2 RPC, 2/2 LPC, K2, 2/2 LC, P1.
Row 40: K1, P8, K4, P8, K1.
Row 41: P1, K4, 2/2 RC, P4, 2/2 LC, K4, P1.
Row 42: K1, P8, K4, P8, K1.
Row 43: P1, K2, 2/2 RC, K2, P4, K2, 2/2 LC, K2, P1.
Row 44: K1, P8, K4, P8, K1.
Row 45: P1, 2/2 RPC, K4, P4, K4, 2/2 LPC, P1.
Rep Rows 2-45 for pattern.

Chart B (flat over 11 sts)
Row 1 (RS): P1, K6, 2/2 RC.
Row 2 and all WS rows: P10, K1.
Row 3: P1, K4, 2/2 RC, K2.
Row 5: P1, K2, 2/2 RC, K4.
Row 7: P1, 2/2 RC, K2, 2/2 RC.
Row 8: Rep Row 2.
Rep Rows 1-8 for pattern.

Chart C (flat over 11 sts)
Row 1 (RS): 2/2 LC, K6, P1.
Row 2 and all WS rows: K1, P10.
Row 3: K2, 2/2 LC, K4, P1.
Row 5: K4, 2/2 LC, K2, P1.
Row 7: 2/2 LC, K2, 2/2 LC, P1.
Row 8: Rep Row 2.
Rep Rows 1-8 for pattern.

DIRECTIONS

Front

Note: Work the full 1–45 rows of Chart A once. Then begin Chart A again from Row 2 (WS) and work through Row 26, 32, or 38, depending on size; neck shaping can begin after any of these rows, so if your row gauge varies from the pattern and you need to adjust body length, simply cont in established pattern and begin neck shaping after one of these three rows.

Hem

With smaller needles, CO 97 (107, 121, 131, 145)(159, 167, 181, 191, 205) sts using preferred cast on for ribbing.
Row 1 (RS): (K1 TBL, P1) to last st, K1 TBL.
Row 2 (WS): (P1 TBL, K1) to last st, P1 TBL.
Rep Rows 1–2 two more times, then rep Row 1 once more.
Next Row (WS): P9 (10, 12, 13, 14)(15, 16, 18, 19, 20), *M1P, P19 (21, 24, 26, 29)(32, 33, 36, 38, 41); rep from * three more times, M1P, P to end. 102 (112, 126, 136, 150)(164, 172, 186, 196, 210) sts.

Body

Switch to larger needles.
Setup Row 1 (RS): K1, P4 (2, 2, 0, 0)(0, 4, 4, 2, 2), PM, (P1, K6) 5 (6, 7, 8, 9)(10, 10, 11, 12, 13) times, PM, work Row 1 of Chart A over next 22 sts, PM, (K6, P1) to last 5 (3, 3, 1, 1)(1, 5, 5, 3, 3) sts, PM, P4 (2, 2, 0, 0)(0, 4, 4, 2, 2), K1.
Setup Row 2 (WS): K to M, (K1, P6) to next M, work Row 2 of Chart A to M, (P6, K1) to M, K to end.

Row 1: K1, P to M, (1/2 RC, 1/2 LC, P1) to M, work next Row of Chart A to M, (1/2 RC, 1/2 LC, P1) to M, P to last st, K1.
Row 2: K to M, (K1, P6) to M, work next row of Chart A to M, (K1, P6) to M, K to end.
Rep Rows 1–2 until body measures 9.5 (9.5, 9.5, 10.25, 10.25)(10.25, 11, 11, 11, 11)" from CO edge.

Armhole Shaping

Row 1 (RS): Removing first M as you come to it, BO 2 (2, 2, 2, 2)(3, 3, 3, 3, 3) sts, work as established to end.
Row 2 (WS): Rep Row 1. 98 (108, 122, 132, 146)(158, 166, 180, 190, 204) sts.
Row 3: K1, SSK, work as established to last 3 sts, K2tog, K1. 2 sts dec.
Row 4: Work as established to end.
Rep Rows 3–4 once more. 94 (104, 118, 128, 142)(154, 162, 176, 186, 200) sts.
From this point forward, sts closest to armhole that can no longer be worked in 1/2 Cable Cross Pattern should be worked in Rev St st.
Cont as established until Row 26 (26, 26, 32, 32)(32, 38, 38, 38, 38) of Chart A.

Neck

Setup Row 1 (RS): Work to 3 sts before center panel M, P1, K2tog, SM, work first row of Chart B over 11 sts, PM, PU the running thread between st just worked and next st on LH needle, K into the front, back, then front again (3 st inc), PM, work first row of Chart C over 11 sts, SM, SSK, P1, work to end as established. 95 (105, 119, 129, 143)(155, 163, 177, 187, 201) sts.

Setup Row 2 (WS): Work to 2 sts before M, K1, P1, SM, work Row 2 of Chart C, SM, K1, P1, K1, SM, work Row 2 of Chart B, SM, P1, K1, work as established to end.

Row 1: Work as established to 3 sts before M, P1, K2tog, SM, work next row of Chart B to M, SM, M1R, work Twisted Rib to next M, M1L, SM, work next row of Chart C to M, SM, SSK, P1, work as established to end.
Row 2: Work as established to M, work next row of Chart C to M, work Twisted Rib to M, incorporating new sts into established pattern, work next row of Chart B to M, work as established to end.
Rep Rows 1–2 until there are 41 (45, 47, 53, 55)(59, 63, 67, 69, 73) sts between Ms in Twisted Rib.

Cont as established, working no additional incs or decs, until armhole measures 7.75 (8.25, 8.75, 9, 9.5)(9.75, 10, 10.5, 11, 11.5)".
Next Row (RS): Work as established to 2 sts before M, P1, K1, SM, work as established to next M, remove M, BO all Twisted Rib sts, remove M, work as established to M, SM, K1, P1, work as established to end. 27 (30, 36, 38, 44)(48, 50, 55, 59, 64) sts remain for each shoulder.
Place remaining left front sts on st holder or scrap yarn.

Right Front

Setup Row (WS): WE as established.
Short Row 1 (RS): Work as established to last 3 sts, W&T.
Short Row 2 (WS): Work in pattern to end.
Short Row 3: Work as established to 5 sts before last wrapped st, W&T.
Short Row 4: Work in pattern to end.
Rep Short Rows 3–4 once more.
Short Row 7: Work as established to 6 sts before last wrapped st, W&T.
Short Row 8: Work in pattern to end.
Rep Short Rows 7–8 another 1 (1, 1, 1, 2)(2, 2, 3, 3, 3) time(s).
Next Row: Work to end, knitting knit sts and purling purled sts while picking up wraps and working them tog with their wrapped sts.
Place sts on st holder or scrap yarn.

Left Front

Join yarn at neck edge.
Short Row 1 (WS): Work as established to last 3 sts, W&T.
Short Row 2 (RS): Work in pattern to end.
Short Row 3: Work as established to 5 sts before last wrapped st, W&T.
Short Row 4: Work in pattern to end.
Rep Short Rows 3–4 once more.
Short Row 7: Work as established to 6 sts before last wrapped st, W&T.
Short Row 8: Work in pattern to end.
Rep Short Rows 7–8 another 1 (1, 1, 1, 2)(2, 2, 3, 3, 3) time(s).
Next Row: Work to end, knitting knit sts and purling purled sts while picking up wraps and working them tog with their wrapped sts.
Place sts on holder or scrap yarn.

Chart A

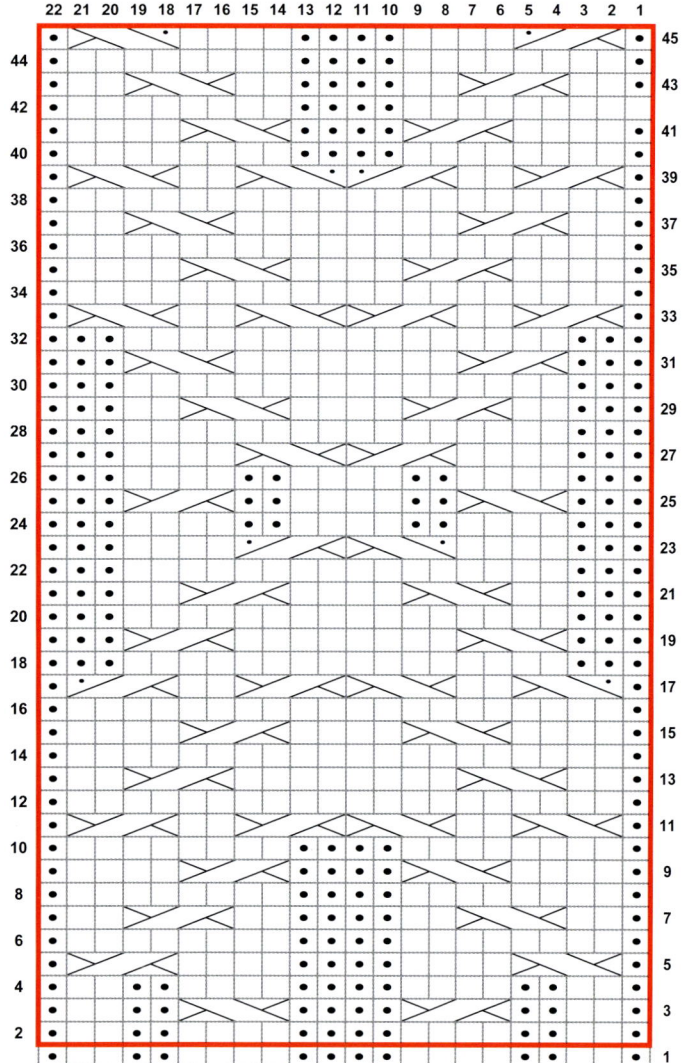

LEGEND

□ **K**
RS: Knit stitch
WS: Purl stitch

● **P**
RS: Purl stitch
WS: Knit stitch

2 over 2 Right Cable (2/2 RC)
Sl2 to CN, hold in back; K2, K2 from CN

2 over 2 Left Cable (2/2 LC)
Sl2 to CN, hold in front; K2, K2 from CN

2 over 2 Right Cable, Purl back (2/2 RPC)
Sl2 to CN, hold in back; K2, P2 from CN

2 over 2 Left Cable, Purl back (2/2 LPC)
Sl2 to CN, hold in front; P2, K2 from CN

☐ **Pattern Repeat**

Chart B

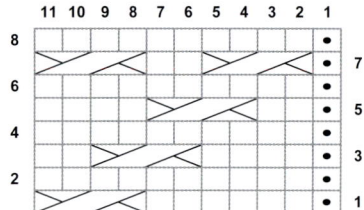

Chart C

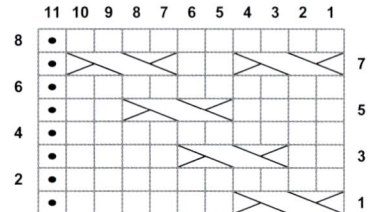

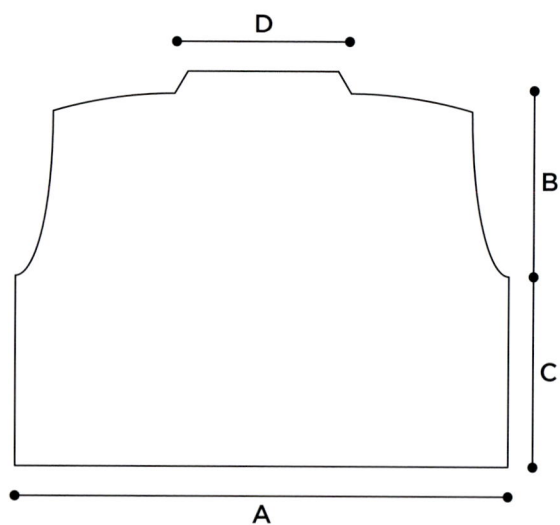

A *chest width* 17 (18.75, 21, 22.75, 25)(27.25, 28.75, 31, 32.75, 35)"
B *armhole depth* 8 (8.5, 9, 9.25, 9.75)(10, 10.25, 10.75, 11.25, 11.75)"
C *body length* 9.5 (9.5, 9.5, 10.25, 10.25)(10.25, 11, 11, 11, 11)"
D *back neck width* 6.75 (7.5, 7.75, 9, 9)(9.5, 10.5, 10.75, 11.75, 12)"

12   Ventisca Slipover

Back

Hem
With smaller needles, CO 97 (109, 121, 133, 145)(157, 169, 181, 193, 205) sts.
Row 1 (RS): (K1 TBL, P1) to last st, K1 TBL.
Row 2 (WS): (P1 TBL, K1) to last st, P1 TBL.
Rep Rows 1-2 two more times, then Rep Row 1 once more.
Next Row (WS): P12 (10, 12, 13, 14, 20, 21, 23, 16, 20), *M1P, P24 (19, 24, 26, 29, 39, 42, 45, 32, 41); rep from * 3 (5, 4, 4, 4)(3, 3, 3, 5, 4) more times, P to end. 101 (115, 126, 138, 150)(161, 173, 185, 199, 210) sts.

Body
Switch to larger needles.
Setup Row (RS): K1, P1 (0, 2, 1, 0)(2, 1, 0, 0, 2), PM, (1/2 RC, 1/2 LC, P1) to last 3 (2, 4, 3, 2)(4, 3, 2, 2, 4) sts, P1, PM, P1 (0, 2, 1, 0)(2, 1, 0, 0, 2), K1.
Row 1 (WS): K1, P to M, K1, (P6, K1) to M, P to last st, K1.
Row 2: K1, P to M, (1/2 RC, 1/2 LC, P1) to 1 st before M, P1, P to last st, K1.
Rep Rows 1-2 until body measures 9.5 (9.5, 9.5, 10.25, 10.25)(10.25, 11, 11, 11, 11)" from CO edge, ending with Row 1.

Armhole Shaping
Row 1 (RS): Removing first M as you come to it, BO 2 (2, 2, 2, 2)(3, 3, 3, 3, 3) sts, work as established to end.
Row 2 (WS): Rep Row 1. 97 (111, 122, 134, 146)(155, 167, 179, 193, 204) sts.
Row 3: K1, SSK, work as established to last 3 sts, K2tog, K1.
Row 4: Work as established to end.
Rep Rows 3-4 once more. 93 (107, 118, 130, 142)(151, 163, 175, 189, 200) sts.
From this point forward, sts closest to armhole that can no longer be worked in 1/2 Cable Cross pattern should be worked in Rev St st.
Cont as established until armhole measures 7.75 (8.25, 8.75, 9, 9.5)(9.75, 10, 10.5, 11, 11.5)".

Size - (-, -, -, -)(54.5, -, -, -, -)" Only
Next Row (RS): K1, M1L, work next 46 sts as established, BO next 57 sts, work as established to last st, M1R, K1.

Sizes 34 (37.5, 42, 45.5, 50)(-, 57.5, 62, 65.5, 70)" Only
Next Row (RS): Work 27 (30, 36, 38, 44)(-, 50, 55, 59, 64) sts as established, BO next 39 (47, 46, 54, 54)(-, 63, 65, 71, 72) sts, work as established to end.

Resume All Sizes
27 (30, 36, 38, 44)(48, 50, 55, 59, 64) remain for each shoulder. Place remaining Right Back sts on holder or scrap yarn.

Left Back
Setup Row (WS): WE as established.
Short Row 1 (RS): Work as established to last 3 sts, W&T.
Short Row 2: Work in pattern to end.
Short Row 3: Work as established to 5 sts before last wrapped st, W&T.
Short Row 4: Work in pattern to end.
Rep Short Rows 3-4 once more.
Short Row 7: Work as established to 6 sts before last wrapped st, W&T.
Short Row 8: Work in pattern to end.
Rep Short Rows 7-8 another 1 (1, 1, 1, 2)(2, 2, 3, 3, 3) time(s).
Next Row: Work to end, knitting knit sts and purling purled sts while picking up wraps and working them tog with their wrapped sts.
Place sts on st holder or scrap yarn.

Right Back
Return held right back sts to needle.
Join yarn at neck edge.
Short Row 1 (WS): Work as established to last 3 sts, W&T.
Short Row 2 (RS): Work in pattern to end.
Short Row 3: Work as established to 5 sts before last wrapped st, W&T.
Short Row 4: Work in pattern to end.
Rep Short Rows 3-4 once more.
Short Row 7: Work as established to 6 sts before last wrapped st, W&T.
Short Row 8: Work in pattern to end.
Rep Short Rows 7-8 another 1 (1, 1, 1, 2)(2, 2, 3, 3, 3) time(s).
Next Row: Work to end, knitting knit sts and purling purled sts while picking up wraps and working them tog with their wrapped sts.
Place held right front sts onto spare needle and join to right back sts using 3-Needle Bind Off.
Rep for opposite shoulder.

Seaming
Blocking front and back pieces before seaming sides is highly recommended.
Using a locking M, pin front and back of one armhole tog. Place a second locking M through both front and back at point where you want side vent to end. Seam front and back tog between Ms using Mattress Stitch.
Rep for opposite side.

Collar
With smaller needle, PU and K: 1 st for each BO st across back neckline, 3 sts for every 4 rows up back left neckline and down front left neckline, 1 st for each BO st across front neckline and 3 sts for every 4 rows up right front neckline and down right back neckline, ending with an even number of sts. (Exact st count is not important.)
Work Twisted Rib for approx 2".
BO loosely.

Armhole Trim
With smaller needle, PU and K: 3 sts for every 4 rows around armhole and 1 st for each BO st at underarm, ending with an even number of sts. Work Twisted Rib for four rows.
BO loosely.

Finishing
Weave in all ends, wash, and block to finished dimensions or to achieve desired results.

PRIMROSE PULLOVER
by Megan Gonzalez

FINISHED MEASUREMENTS
28 (32, 36, 40, 44)(48, 52, 56, 60)" finished chest circumference; meant to be worn with 0–2" positive ease
Samples are 36/44"; models are 34.5/43"

YARN
High Desert™ (worsted weight, 100% American Wool; 113 yards/50g): 10 (11, 12, 13, 15)(16, 18, 20, 21) hanks
Size 36" sample Campion 29484
Size 44" sample Chaps Heather 29603

NEEDLES
US 8 (5mm) 32–40" circular needles, or size to obtain gauge

US 6 (4mm) DPNs or two circular needles for two circulars technique or 32" or longer circular needles for Magic Loop technique, or two sizes smaller than size used to obtain gauge

NOTIONS
Yarn Needle
Stitch Markers
Two Cable Needles
Stitch Holders or Scrap Yarn

GAUGE
19 sts and 28 rnds = 4" in Stockinette Stitch in the round, blocked
Cable Chart B: 18 sts = 2.5" / 38 rnds = 4.75"

For pattern support, contact megan@nurtureknitwear.com

Primrose Pullover

Notes:

"Delicate, yet hardy" is the perfect description for the four-pointed primrose used to repopulate barren prairies. In the Primrose pullover, a delicate motif of flowers and vines twines up flat lands of stockinette to bloom in all its glory in a stunning shoulder motif.

This wardrobe staple is a raglan worked from the top down. The hexagonal shoulder cable is worked out of the collar ribbing and transitions into the Primrose & Vines cable, which twists down the sleeves and sides, into the hem and cuff ribbing. With loads of stockinette in between cable columns, Primrose is a relaxing knit with striking style.

Charts are worked in the round; read each chart row from right to left as a RS row.

Slip all markers when they are reached, unless otherwise indicated.

End sleeves and body on a Rnd 10, 12, 22, or 24 of Chart B for a smooth fade into ribbing.

Tubular Cast On
View a photo tutorial at: tutorials.knitpicks.com/tubular-cast-on.

Tubular Bind Off
View a photo tutorial at: knitpicks.com/learning-center/tubular-bind-off.

KFBF (Knit Front, Back, Front)
Knit into front, then back, then front of same stitch. 2 sts inc.

PFBF (Purl Front, Back, Front)
Purl into front, then back, then front of same stitch. 2 sts inc.

LPT (Left Twist, Purl back)
Sl1 to CN, hold in front; P1, K1 from CN.

RPT (Right Twist, Purl back)
Sl1 to CN, hold in back; K1, P1 from CN.

2/2/2 LPC (2 over 2 over 2 Left Cable, Purl center)
Sl2 to CN, hold in front; Sl2 to second CN, hold in back; K2, P2 from back CN, K2 from front CN.

2/2/2 RPC (2 over 2 over 2 Right Cable, Purl center)
Sl4 sts to CN, hold in back; K2, Sl2 left-most sts from CN to LH needle, hold CN in front; P2 from LH needle; K2 from CN.

2/2 LC (2 over 2 Left Cable)
Sl2 to CN, hold in front; K2, K2 from CN.

2/2 LPC (2 over 2 Left Cable, Purl back)
Sl2 to CN, hold in front; P2, K2 from CN.

2/2 RC (2 over 2 Right Cable)
Sl2 to CN, hold in back; K2, K2 from CN.

2/2 RPC (2 over 2 Right Cable, Purl back)
Sl2 to CN, hold in back; K2, P2 from CN.

Chart A (in the round over an increasing st count)
Rnd 1: PFBF, P1, 2/2/2 RPC, P1, PFBF. 14 sts.
Rnd 2: P4, K2, P2, K2, P4.
Rnd 3: PFBF, P1, 2/2 RPC, P2, 2/2 LPC, P1, PFBF. 18 sts.
Rnd 4: P4, K2, P6, K2, P4.
Rnd 5: PFBF, P1, 2/2 RPC, P6, 2/2 LPC, P1, PFBF. 22 sts.
Rnd 6: P4, K2, P10, K2, P4.
Rnd 7: PFBF, P1, 2/2 RC, P10, 2/2 LC, P1, PFBF. 26 sts.
Rnd 8: P4, K4, P10, K4, P4.
Rnd 9: PFBF, P1, 2/2 RPC, K2, P10, K2, 2/2 LPC, P1, PFBF. 30 sts.
Rnd 10: P4, K2, P2, K2, P10, K2, P2, K2, P4.
Rnd 11: PFBF, P1, 2/2 RC, P2, 2/2 LPC, P6, 2/2 RPC, P2, 2/2 LC, P1, PFBF. 34 sts.
Rnd 12: P4, K4, P4, K2, P6, K2, P4, K4, P4.
Rnd 13: PFBF, P1, 2/2 RPC, K2, P4, 2/2 LPC, P2, 2/2 RPC, P4, K2, 2/2 LPC, P1, PFBF. 38 sts.
Rnd 14: P4, K2, P2, K2, (P6, K2, P2, K2) two times, P4.
Rnd 15: PFBF, P1, 2/2 RPC, P2, K2, P6, 2/2/2 RPC, P6, K2, P2, 2/2 LPC, P1, PFBF. 42 sts.
Rnd 16: (P4, K2) two times, P6, K2, P2, K2, P6, (K2, P4) two times.
Rnd 17: PFBF, P1, 2/2 RPC, P4, K2, P4, 2/2 RPC, P2, 2/2 LPC, P4, K2, P4, 2/2 LPC, P1, PFBF. 46 sts.
Rnd 18: (P4, K2, P6, K2) three times, P4.
Rnd 19: PFBF, P1, 2/2 RC, P6, K2, P2, 2/2 RPC, P6, 2/2 LPC, P2, K2, P6, 2/2 LC, P1, PFBF. 50 sts.
Rnd 20: P4, K4, P6, K2, P2, K2, P10, K2, P2, K2, P6, K4, P4.
Rnd 21: P2, 2/2 RPC, K2, P6, 2/2/2 RPC, P10, 2/2/2 LPC, P6, K2, 2/2 LPC, P2.
Rnd 22: (P2, K2) two times, P6, K2, P2, K2, P10, K2, P2, K2, P6, (K2, P2) two times.
Rnd 23: (P2, K2) two times, P4, 2/2 RC, P2, 2/2 LC, P6, 2/2 RC, P2, 2/2 LC, P4, (K2, P2) two times.
Rnd 24: (P2, K2) two times, P4, K4, P4, K4, P6, K4, P2, K4, P4, (K2, P2) two times.
Rnd 25: (P2, K2) two times, (P2, 2/2 RPC, K2, P2, K2, 2/2 LPC) two times, (P2, K2) two times, P2.
Rnds 26-28: (P2, K2) twelve times, P2.
Rnd 29: P2, K2, P2, (K2, P2, K2, 2/2 RPC, P2, 2/2 LPC) two times, (K2, P2) three times.
Rnd 30: (P2, K2) two times, (P2, K4, P6, K4) two times, (P2, K2) two times, P2.
Rnd 31: (P2, K2) two times, (P2, 2/2 RPC, P6, 2/2 LPC) two times, (P2, K2) two times, P2.
Rnd 32: P2, K2, P2, (K2, P2, K2, P10) two times, (K2, P2) three times.
Rnd 33: (P2, K2) three times, P10, 2/2/2 RPC, P10, (K2, P2) three times.
Rnd 34: Rep Rnd 32.
Rnd 35: (P2, K2) two times, (P2, 2/2 LC, P6, 2/2 RC) two times, (P2, K2) two times, P2.
Rnd 36: Rep Rnd 30.
Rnd 37: P2, K2, P2, (K2, P2, K2, 2/2 LPC, P2, 2/2 RPC) two times, (K2, P2) three times.

Rnds 38-40: (P2, K2) twelve times, P2.
Rnd 41: (P2, K2) two times, (P2, 2/2 LPC, K2, P2, K2, 2/2 RPC) two times, (P2, K2) two times, P2.
Rnd 42: Rep Rnd 24.
Rnd 43: (P2, K2) two times, P4, 2/2 LPC, P2, 2/2 RPC, P6, 2/2 LPC, P2, 2/2 RPC, P4, (K2, P2) two times.
Rnd 44: Rep Rnd 22.
Rnd 45: P2, 2/2 LPC, K2, P6, 2/2/2 LPC, P10, 2/2/2 RPC, P6, K2, 2/2 RPC, P2.
Rnd 46: Rep Rnd 20.
Rnd 47 (use special rnd instructions in *Directions*): (K2, P2, 2/2 LPC, P6) two times, 2/2 RPC, P2, K2, P6, 2/2 RPC, P2, K2.
Rnd 48: (K2, P4, K2, P6) three times, K2, P4, K2.
Rnd 49: 2/2 LC, P2, 2/2 LPC, P4, K2, P4, 2/2 LPC, P2, 2/2 RPC, P4, K2, P4, 2/2 RPC, P2, 2/2 RC.
Rnd 50: K4, (P4, K2) two times, P6, K2, P2, K2, P6, (K2, P4) two times, K4.
Rnd 51: K2, 2/2 LC, P2, 2/2 LPC, P2, K2, P6, 2/2/2 RPC, P6, K2, P2, 2/2 RPC, P2, 2/2 RC, K2.
Rnd 52: K6, P4, K2, P2, K2, (P6, K2, P2, K2) two times, P4, K6.
Rnd 53: K4, 2/2 LC, P2, 2/2 LPC, K2, P4, 2/2 RPC, P2, 2/2 LPC, P4, K2, 2/2 RPC, P2, 2/2 RC, K4.
Rnd 54: K8, P4, K4, P4, K2, P6, K2, P4, K4, P4, K8.
Rnd 55: K6, 2/2 LC, P2, 2/2 LPC, P2, 2/2 RPC, P6, 2/2 LPC, P2, 2/2 RPC, P2, 2/2 RC, K6.
Rnd 56: K10, P4, K2, P2, K2, P10, K2, P2, K2, P4, K10.
Rnd 57: K8, 2/2 LC, P2, 2/2 LPC, K2, P10, K2, 2/2 RPC, P2, 2/2 RC, K8.
Rnd 58: K12, P4, K4, P10, K4, P4, K12.
Rnd 59: K10, 2/2 LC, P2, 2/2 LPC, P10, 2/2 RPC, P2, 2/2 RC, K10.
Rnd 60: K14, P4, K2, P10, K2, P4, K14.
Rnd 61: K12, 2/2 LC, P2, 2/2 LPC, P6, 2/2 RPC, P2, 2/2 RC, K12.
Rnd 62: K16, P4, K2, P6, K2, P4, K16.
Rnd 63: K16, P4, 2/2 LPC, P2, 2/2 RPC, P4, K16.
Rnd 64: K16, P6, K2, P2, K2, P6, K16.
Rnd 65: K16, P6, 2/2/2 RPC, P6, K16.
Rnd 66: Rep Rnd 64.

Chart B (in the round over 18 sts)
Rnd 1: P4, 2/2 RPC, P2, 2/2 LPC, P4.
Rnd 2: P4, K2, P6, K2, P4.
Rnd 3: P2, 2/2 RPC, P6, 2/2 LPC, P2.
Rnds 4-6: P2, K2, P10, K2, P2.
Rnd 7: P2, 2/2 LC, P6, 2/2 RC, P2.
Rnd 8: P2, K4, P6, K4, P2.
Rnd 9: P2, K2, 2/2 LPC, P2, 2/2 RPC, K2, P2.
Rnds 10-12: (P2, K2) four times, P2.
Rnd 13: P2, 2/2 LPC, K2, P2, K2, 2/2 RPC, P2.
Rnd 14: P4, K4, P2, K4, P4.
Rnd 15: P4, 2/2 LPC, P2, 2/2 RPC, P4.
Rnd 16: P6, K2, P2, K2, P6.
Rnd 17: P6, 2/2/2 RPC, P6.
Rnd 18: Rep Rnd 16.
Rnd 19: P4, 2/2 RC, P2, 2/2 LC, P4.
Rnd 20: Rep Rnd 14.
Rnd 21: P2, 2/2 RPC, K2, P2, K2, 2/2 LPC, P2.
Rnds 22-24: (P2, K2) four times, P2.
Rnd 25: P2, K2, 2/2 RPC, P2, 2/2 LPC, K2, P2.
Rnd 26: Rep Rnd 8.
Rnd 27: Rep Rnd 3.
Rnds 28-30: P2, K2, P10, K2, P2.
Rnd 31: P2, 2/2 LPC, P6, 2/2 RPC, P2.
Rnd 32: Rep Rnd 2.
Rnds 33-36: Rep Rnds 15-18.
Rep Rnds 1-36 for pattern.

Chart C—Sizes 28 (32, 36, -, -)(-, -, -, -)" Only (in the round over 20 sts; pattern placement and st count shift in Rnd 6, see *Directions*)
Rnd 1: K4, RPT, P1, K2, P2, K2, P1, LPT, K4.
Rnd 2: K3, RPT, P2, K2, P2, K2, P2, LPT, K3.
Rnd 3: K2, RPT, P1, 2/2 RPC, P2, 2/2 LPC, P1, LPT, K2.
Rnd 4: K1, RPT, P2, K2, P6, K2, P2, LPT, K1.
Rnd 5: RPT, P1, 2/2 RPC, P6, 2/2 LPC, P1, LPT.
Rnd 6: P2, K2, P10, K2, P2. 18 sts.

Chart C—Sizes - (-, -, 40, 44)(48, -, -, -)" Only (in the round over 20 sts; pattern placement and st count shift in Rnd 6, see *Directions*)
Rnd 1: K3, RPT, (P2, K2) two times, P2, LPT, K3.
Rnd 2: K2, RPT, P3, K2, P2, K2, P3, LPT, K2.
Rnd 3: K1, RPT, P2, 2/2 RPC, P2, 2/2 LPC, P2, LPT, K1.
Rnd 4: RPT, P3, K2, P6, K2, P3, LPT.
Rnd 5: K1, P2, 2/2 RPC, P6, 2/2 LPC, P2, K1.
Rnd 6: P2, K2, P10, K2, P2. 18 sts.

Chart C—Sizes - (-, -, -, -)(-, 52, 56, 60)" Only (in the round over 20 sts; pattern placement and st count shift in Rnd 6, see *Directions*)
Rnd 1: K2, RPT, P3, K2, P2, K2, P3, LPT, K2.
Rnd 2: K1, RPT, P4, K2, P2, K2, P4, LPT, K1.
Rnd 3: RPT, P3, 2/2 RPC, P2, 2/2 LPC, P3, LPT.
Rnd 4: K1, P4, K2, P6, K2, P4, K1.
Rnd 5: K1, P2, 2/2 RPC, P6, 2/2 LPC, P2, K1.
Rnd 6: P2, K2, P10, K2, P2. 18 sts.

DIRECTIONS

Collar
With smaller circular needles, CO 88 (88, 96, 96, 104)(104, 104, 104, 112) sts using Tubular Cast On or other stretchy method. Join to work in the rnd, being careful not to twist sts; PM for BOR.
Work 2x2 Rib, beginning with K2, until piece measures 1" from CO edge.

Yoke
Switch to larger needles.
Setup Rnd: K6, PM, (P2, K2) two times, P2, PM, K34 (34, 38, 38, 42)(42, 42, 42, 46), PM, (P2, K2) two times, P2, PM, K to end.
Rnds 1-20: (K to M, work Chart A to M) two times, K to end. 168 (168, 176, 176, 184)(184, 184, 184, 192) sts.
Rnd 21: (K to 2 sts before M, M1R, K2, work Chart A to M, K2, M1L) two times, K to end. 4 sts inc.
Rnd 22: (K to M, work Chart A to M) two times, K to end.

Rep Rnds 21-22 another 13 (15, 17, 18, 17)(15, 13, 10, 13) times—*substitute the special instructions below for Chart Rnd 47 ONLY, whenever it's reached (for Size 28" only, this will be in the Lower Yoke). 224 (232, 248, 252, 256)(248, 240, 228, 248) sts.
***Rnd 47:** (K to 2 sts before M, M1R, 2/2 LC, always taking care to replace M in center of cross, work Chart A to 2 sts before M, 2/2 RC, M1L) two times, K to end. 4 sts inc.

Lower Yoke
In Rnd 1, a second set of markers will be added. The new set of Ms will be for the raglan inc lines. Existing Ms are chart Ms.
Note: After completing Chart A, (work inc pattern as established to chart M, remove M, K16, PM, work Chart B, PM, K16, remove M) two times. Cont working Chart B for remaining Yoke and/or sleeves.
Rnd 1: (K to 2 sts before M, M1R, K1, PM, K1, M1L, SM, work Chart A to M, SM, M1R, K1, PM, K1, M1L) two times, K to end. 232 (240, 256, 260, 264)(256, 248, 236, 256) sts.
Rnds 2: ([K to M] two times, work Chart A or B to M, K to M) two times, K to end.
Rnd 3: (K to 1 st before M, M1R, K1, SM, K1, M1L, K to M, work Chart A or B to M, K to 1 st before M, M1R, K1, SM, K1, M1L) two times, K to end. 8 sts inc.
Rnd 4: Rep Rnd 2.
Rep Rnds 3-4 another 0 (3, 4, 5, 9)(9, 10, 12, 10) times. 240 (272, 296, 308, 344)(336, 336, 340, 344) sts.

Sizes - (-, -, 40, -)(48, 52, 56, 60)" Only
Next Rnd: (K to 2 sts before M, KFBF, K1, SM, K1, M1L, K to M, work Chart A or B to M, K to 1 st before M, M1R, K1, SM, K1, KFBF) two times, K to end. 12 sts inc.
Next Rnd: ([K to M] two times, work Chart A or B to M, K to M) two times, K to end.
Rep those two rnds - (-, -, 0, -)(3, 5, 8, 9) more times. - (-, -, 320, -)(384, 408, 448, 464) sts.

Resume All Sizes
Work in St st and cable pattern as established until yoke measures 10.5 (10.5, 10.5, 11, 11.5)(12, 12.5, 13, 13.5)" from CO edge, measuring over cables.
Armhole Division: *K to M, SM, K1, place 54 (60, 62, 66, 72)(80, 86, 96, 94) sts and chart Ms on st holder or scrap yarn, CO 6 (6, 6, 8, 8)(8, 10, 10, 10) sts, K1, remove M; rep from * once more, K to end. 144 (164, 184, 204, 216)(240, 256, 276, 296) sts.

Body
Rnd 1: *K to 6 (6, 6, 5, 5)(5, 4, 4, 4) sts before M, PM, work Chart C (remove original M when reached), PM; rep from * once more, K to end.
Rnds 2-5: (K to M, work Chart C to M) two times, K to end.
Rnd 6: (K to M, remove M, K1, PM, work Chart C to 1 st before M, PM, K1, remove M) two times, K to end.
Rnd 7: (K to M, work Chart B beginning with Rnd 5 to M) two times, K to end.
Rnd 8: (K to M, work Chart B as established to M) two times, K to end.
Rep Rnd 8 until body measures 13.5" from armhole division, or 2" shorter than desired length.

Hem
Sizes 28 (-, 36, -, 44)(48, 52, -, 60)" Only
Setup Rnd: Remove BOR M, K to 2 sts before M, place BOR M; using smaller needles, (K2, P2) to new BOR, removing all additional Ms.

Sizes - (32, -, 40, -)(-, -, 56, -)" Only
Setup Rnd: Remove BOR M, K to 1 st before M, place BOR M; using smaller needles, M1R, K1, remove M, (P2, K2) to 2 sts before M, P2, remove M, K1, M1L, (P2, K2) to 3 sts before M, P2, M1R, K1, remove M, (P2, K2) to 2 sts before M, P2, remove M, K1, M1L, (K2, P2) to new BOR. - (168, -, 208, -)(-, -, 280, -) sts.

Resume All Sizes
Work 2x2 Rib as established for 2".
BO in pattern using Tubular Bind Off or other stretchy method.

Sleeves (make two the same)
Starting at center of underarm and using larger needles, PU and K 3 (3, 3, 4, 4)(4, 5, 5, 5) sts, K to M, work Chart B, K to CO, PU and K 3 (3, 3, 4, 4)(4, 5, 5, 5) sts. 60 (66, 68, 74, 80)(88, 96, 106, 104) sts.
Sleeve Rnd: K to M, work Chart B, K to end.
Dec Rnd: K1, SSK, K to M, work Chart B, K to last 3 sts, K2tog, K1. 2 sts dec.
Rep Dec Rnd every 11(8, 9, 7, 6)(5, 4, 4, 4) rnds 9 (12, 11, 14, 17)(19, 23, 26, 25) more times. 40 (40, 44, 44, 44)(48, 48, 52, 52).

Work as established until sleeve measures 14.5 (15, 15, 15.5, 15.5)(16, 16, 16.5, 16.5)". Switch to smaller needles.

Sizes 28 (32, -, -, -)(48, 52, -, -)" Only
Cuff Rnd: P1, (K2, P2) to last 3 sts, K2, P1.

Sizes - (-, 36, 40, 44)(-, -, 56, 60)" Only
Cuff Rnd: K1, (P2, K2) to last 3 sts, P2, K1.

Resume All Sizes
Rep Cuff Rnd for 2".
BO in pattern using Tubular Bind Off or other stretchy method.

Finishing
Weave in ends, wash, and block to measurements or to achieve desired results.

20   Primrose Pullover

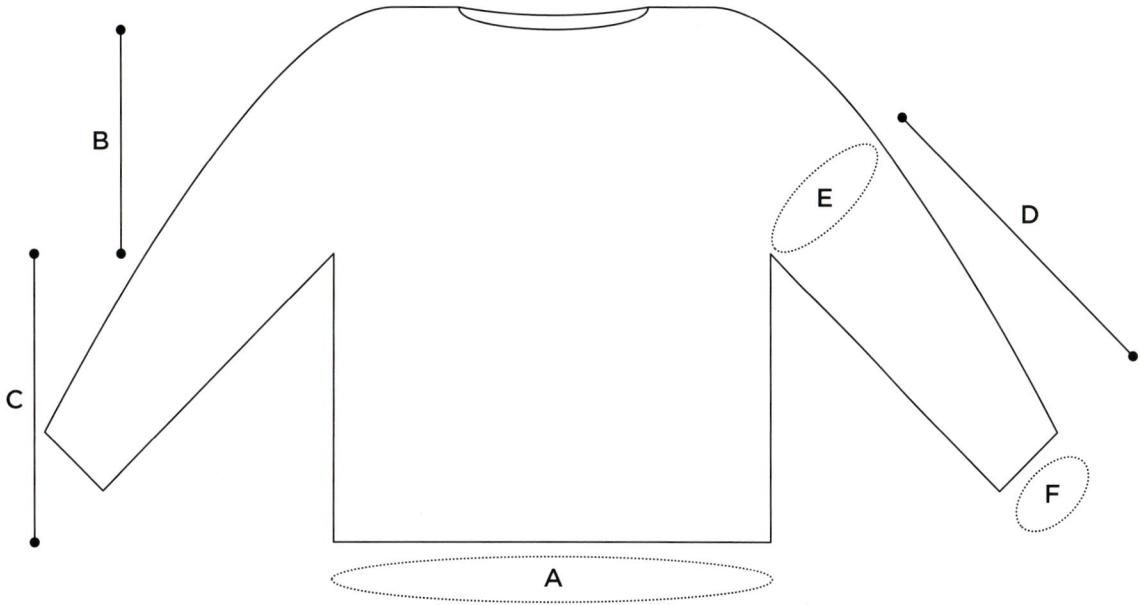

- **A** *chest circumference* 28 (32, 36, 40, 44)(48, 52, 56, 60)"
- **B** *yoke depth* 10.5 (10.5, 10.5, 11, 11.5)(12, 12.5, 13, 13.5)"
- **C** *body length to underarm* 15.5"
- **D** *sleeve length* 16.5 (17, 17, 17.5, 17.5)(18, 18, 18.5, 18.5)"
- **E** *upper arm circumference* 11.25 (12.5, 13, 14.25, 15.5)(17.25, 19, 21, 20.5)"
- **F** *cuff circumference* 7.25 (7.25, 8, 8, 8)(9, 9, 9.75, 9.75)"

Chart A

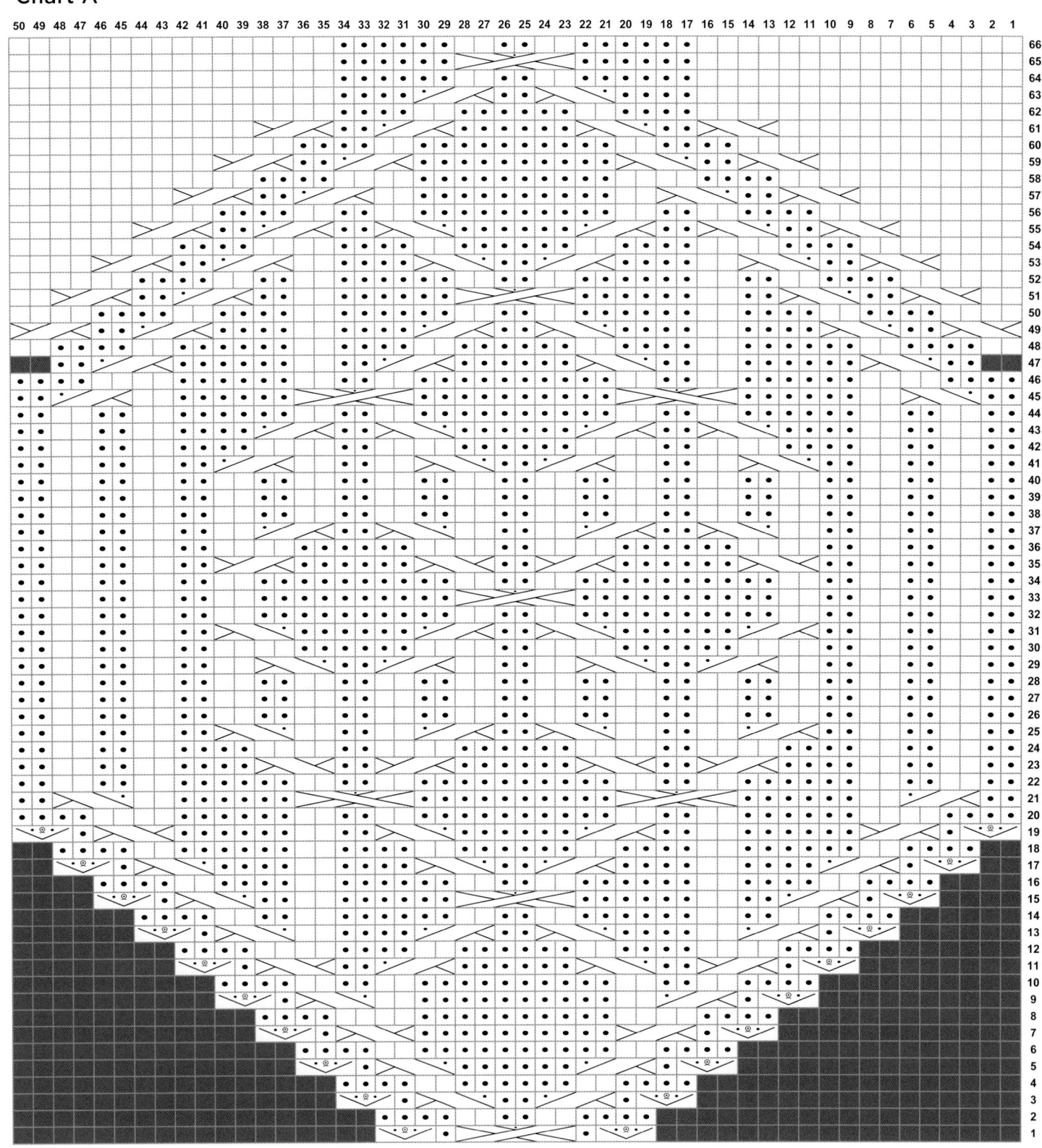

Chart B

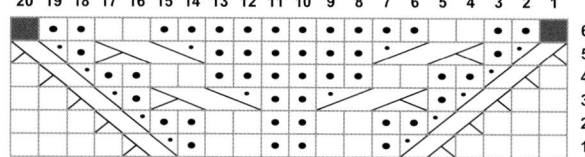

Chart C—Sizes 28 (32, 36, -, -)(-, -, -, -)"

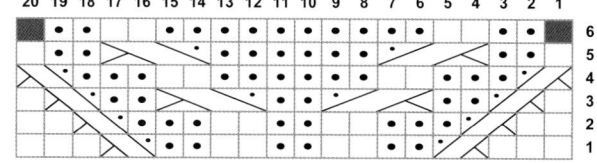

Chart C—Sizes - (-, -, 40, 44)(48, -, -, -)"

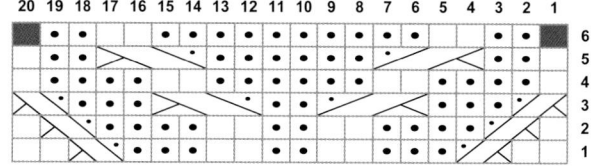

Chart C—Sizes - (-, -, -, -)(-, 52, 56, 60)"

LEGEND

■ **No Stitch**
Placeholder—no stitch made

☐ **Knit Stitch**

• **Purl Stitch**

PFBF
Purl into front, then back, then front of same stitch

 **Right Twist, Purl back (RPT)**
Sl1 to CN, hold in back; K1, P1 from CN

 **Left Twist, Purl back (LPT)**
Sl1 to CN, hold in front; P1, K1 from CN

 **2 over 2 Right Cable (2/2 RC)**
Sl2 to CN, hold in back; K2, K2 from CN

 **2 over 2 Left Cable (2/2 LC)**
Sl2 to CN, hold in front; K2, K2 from CN

2 over 2 Right Cable, Purl back (2/2 RPC)
Sl2 to CN, hold in back; K2, P2 from CN

2 over 2 Left Cable, Purl back (2/2 LPC)
Sl2 to CN, hold in front; P2, K2 from CN

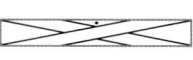 **2 over 2 over 2 Right Cable, Purl center (2/2/2 RPC)**
Sl4 sts to CN, hold in back; K2, Sl2 left-most sts from CN to LH needle, hold CN in front; P2 from LH needle; K2 from CN

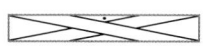 **2 over 2 over 2 Left Cable, Purl center (2/2/2 LPC)**
Sl2 to CN, hold in front; Sl2 to second CN, hold in back; K2, P2 from back CN, K2 from front CN

FLYING TRAPEZE SHAWL
by Holli Yeoh

FINISHED MEASUREMENTS
11.5 (22.5, 33.5, 44.5)" width (at wide edge) × 69 (60, 78, 91)" length, not including optional tassels
Sample is 78" long

YARN
Gloss™ (fingering weight, 70% Merino Wool, 30% Silk; 220 yards/50g): Harvest 28602, 3 (5, 9, 15) hanks

NEEDLES
US 4 (3.5mm) circular needles (24" for smaller sizes; 32" for larger sizes), or size to obtain gauge

NOTIONS
Yarn Needle
Stitch Markers

GAUGE
24 sts and 28 rows = 4" in Stockinette Stitch, hard blocked
25-st repeat = 4" and three 12-row repeats = 5.25" in Cable Panel, hard blocked (gauge is not crucial, but it will affect finished size and yardage requirements); see *Notes* for Cable Panel swatch directions

For pattern support, contact info@holliyeoh.com

Flying Trapeze Shawl

Notes:
With a background of dropped stitches, these cables seem to catch each other in mid-air like a great trapeze act. The asymmetric trapezoid shape adds even more to the impression of swinging energy, finished with tassels for a little razzle-dazzle.

Choose the right level of drama: the pattern offers three shawl sizes and one scarf size, all worked from the narrow to the wide end, with panel(s) of drop-stitch cables on a ground of Reverse Stockinette Stitch divided by ribbing. Simple stretchy cast-on and bind-off edges allow the option of blocking the shawl with either scalloped or straight ends.

To ease dropping the sts down through the cables, they are dropped every 12 rows at the cable cross. It is possible, but perhaps unnecessarily fiddly, to drop them at the very end if preferred.

Charts are worked flat; read RS rows (odd numbers) from right to left, and WS rows (even numbers) from left to right.

Modification Notes
The scarf or shawl may be worked to any length, allowing you to customize the piece to the amount of yarn available. Stop increasing about 12-20 rows before binding off. The Cable Panel looks best when the last row worked before the final Drop Row is four rows after the 3/3/3 LPCD cable cross.

Cable Panel Swatch
Using Old Norwegian Cast On or preferred stretchy cast on method, CO 45 sts.
Following instructions for smallest size and omitting incs, work Rows 1-12 three times, then work Rows 13-22 one time. Using Stretchy Bind Off method, BO all sts.
To block swatch, soak in luke warm water for 20 minutes with some wool wash. Press excess water out in a towel. Hard block swatch by stretching and pinning it out to its fullest extent and allow to dry thoroughly. Once dry, unpin and leave on a smooth surface to relax for at least 24 hours. Toss swatch back and forth between hands several times to encourage the relaxing process. Hard blocked lace may continue to relax for several days after it has dried or as the weather becomes more humid.
Measure width of cable panel from outer edges of knit sts on either side at the approx Row 5 location in pattern repeat. Measure row gauge from lower-most cable cross (first occurrence of Row 5) to upper-most cable cross (Row 17).

Old Norwegian Cast On
This cast on method is very similar to the Long Tail Cast On method but incorporates an extra twist in the yarn that helps make the cast on stretchier.
Step 1: Begin by setting up the yarn in your hand the same way as for the Long Tail Cast On; place a slip knot on your needle and hold it in your right hand with the ends hanging down from the slip knot and the tail end closest to you.

Step 2: Pinch the thumb and forefinger on your left hand together and insert them between the dangling strands, then grasp the strands with the remaining three fingers of the left hand, holding them in your fist. Open up the thumb and forefinger and angle your hand so the palm faces up. The yarn should be in a V shape with the tail looped around the thumb and the yarn leading to the ball around the forefinger.
Step 3: Going from front to back, move the needle underneath both strands of the thumb loop yarn. Lift the needle tip high enough so it can then dive down into the center of the thumb loop, then move the needle point towards you, and then back towards the center of the hand. The loop of yarn around the thumb should now have a twist in it.
Step 4: Move the needle over the closest strand on the forefinger and down behind it to wrap it around the needle.
Step 5: Dip the thumb into the center of the fist to open up the loop on the thumb. Dip the needle down into the thumb loop and then towards yourself.
Step 6: Let the thumb loop slip off the thumb and reposition the yarn around the thumb without letting go of the yarn in your fingers. Spread out the thumb to tighten the slack around the base of the stitch.
Repeat Steps 3-6 until the required number of stitches have been cast on, counting the slip knot as the first stitch.

3/3/3 LPCD (3 over 3 over 3 Left Cable with Drop sts, Purl back center)
Sl6 to CN, hold in front; K1, drop 1, YO, K1, Sl last 3 sts from CN to LH needle; P3, (K1, drop 1, YO, K1) from CN.

3/3/3 RPC (3 over 3 over 3 Right Cable, Purl back center)
Sl6 to CN, hold in back; K1, P1, K1, Sl last 3 sts from CN to LH needle; P3, (K1, P1, K1) from CN.

Cable Panel (flat over 27 sts, decreased to 25 sts on Row 1, decreased to 23 sts on Row 22)
Setup Row (WS): P1, K1, P1, K3, P1, K1, P2tog, YO, P2tog, K3, P2tog, YO, P2tog, K1, P1, K3, P1, K1, P1. 25 sts.
Row 1 (RS): K1, P1, K1, P3, K1, (P1, K1 TBL) two times, P3, (K1 TBL, P1) two times, K1, P3, K1, P1, K1.
Row 2: P1, K1, P1, K3, P1, (K1, P1 TBL) two times, K3, (P1 TBL, K1) two times, P1, K3, P1, K1, P1.
Rows 3-4: Rep Rows 1-2.
Row 5: K1, P1, K1, P3, K1, P1, 3/3/3 LPCD, P1, K1, P3, K1, P1, K1.
Row 6: Rep Row 2.
Rows 7-10: Rep Rows 1-4.
Row 11: 3/3/3 RPC, P1, K1 TBL, P3, K1 TBL, P1, 3/3/3 RPC.
Row 12: Rep Row 2.
Rep Rows 1-12 for pattern.
Rows 13-21: Rep Rows 1-9.
Row 22: P1, K1, P1, K3, P1, K1, P1 TBL, drop st, P1 TBL, K3, P1 TBL, drop st, P1 TBL, K1, P1, K3, P1, K1, P1. 23 sts.

LEGEND

K
RS: Knit stitch
WS: Purl stitch

P
RS: Purl stitch
WS: Knit stitch

K TBL
RS: Knit stitch through the back loop
WS: Purl stitch through the back loop

YO
Yarn over

P2tog on WS
WS: Purl 2 stitches together as one stitch

3 over 3 over 3 Left Cable with Drop sts, Purl back center (3/3/3 LPCD)
Sl6 to CN, hold in front; K1, drop 1, YO, K1, Sl last 3 sts from CN to LH needle; P3, (K1, drop 1, YO, K1) from CN

3 over 3 over 3 Right Cable, Purl back center (3/3/3 RPC)
Sl6 to CN, hold in back; K1, P1, K1, Sl last 3 sts from CN to LH needle; P3, (K1, P1, K1) from CN

Drop Stitch

Pattern Repeat

DIRECTIONS

Using Old Norwegian Cast On or preferred stretchy cast on method, CO 45 (85, 125, 165) sts.
Setup Row (WS): (P1, K1) two times, *P1, K4, work Setup Row of Cable Panel from chart or written instructions, PM, K4, PM, (P1, K1) two times; rep from * 0 (1, 2, 3) more time(s), WYIF Sl1 P-wise. 2 (4, 6, 8) Ms. 43 (81, 119, 157) sts.
Row 1 (RS): (K1, P1) two times, *K1, P to next M, work Row 1 of Cable Panel, P4, (K1, P1) two times; rep from * 0 (1, 2, 3) more time(s), WYIB Sl1 K-wise.
Row 2: (P1, K1) two times, *P1, K4, work Row 2 of Cable Panel, K to next M, (P1, K1) two times; rep from * 0 (1, 2, 3) more time(s), WYIF Sl1 P-wise.

Pattern is established. Rep Rows 1-12 of Cable Panel throughout while following shaping instructions as follows. After shaping is complete, Rows 13-22 of Cable Panel will be worked.

Work 13 (11, 15, 17) more rows in pattern as established, being sure to rep Rows 1-12 of Cable Panel, ending with a RS row.

Inc Row (WS): *Work in pattern to next M, then work to 1 st before following M, LLI, K1, SM; rep from * 0 (1, 2, 3) more time(s), work in pattern to end. 1 (2, 3, 4) sts inc. Work one RS row as established.

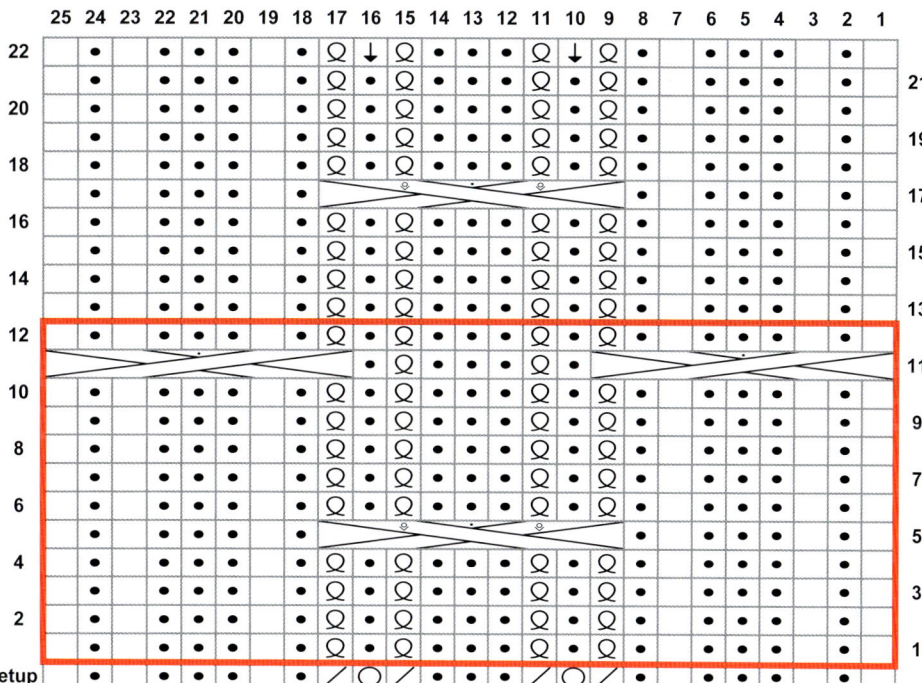

Cable Panel

Rep Inc Row every 14 (12, 16, 18) rows 17 (13, 15, 5) more times. 61 (109, 167, 181) sts.
Rep Inc Row every 16 (14, 18, 20) rows 12 (16, 14, 24) times, ending with a WS row. 73 (141, 209, 277) sts.
Work as established through Row 21 of Cable Panel—19 (11, 15, 19) more rows, ending with a RS row.
Final Drop Row (WS): (P1, K1) two times, *P1, K4, work Row 22 of Cable Panel, K to next M, (P1, K1) two times; rep from * 0 (1, 2, 3) more time(s), WYIF Sl1 P-wise. 71 (137, 203, 269) sts.
Using Stretchy Bind Off method, BO all sts.

Finishing

Weave in ends but do not trim until after blocking is complete.

To block, pin wet shawl stretching it out to its fullest extent. Place pins or blocking wires at transition between edge ribbing and Rev St st so ribbing isn't stretched out. Along wide end, pin out ribbed spines and edges (referring to diagram for pinning locations), allowing Rev St st and Cable Panel sections to relax and create a scalloped edge. Allow to dry. After unpinning, shawl will relax to the finished dimensions.

Trim woven in ends.

Tassels

Make 3 (5, 7, 9) tassels as follows.

Step 1: Wind yarn around a 3" piece of cardboard 30 times.

Step 2: Slide an 8" length of yarn under all the wraps and tie a tight knot at one edge of the card securing all the wraps. Do not cut tails as they'll be used to sew to shawl.

Step 3: Cut the wraps free of the card at the opposite edge of the cardboard from the knot.

Step 4: About 0.5" from the tied end, wrap a 16" length of yarn tightly around the tassel several times and tie it securely.

Step 5: To hide the knot, thread the tails of the knot onto a needle and pass the needle downwards through the bound section towards the cut ends and trim.

Use tail ends to sew tassels to points at wide end of shawl.

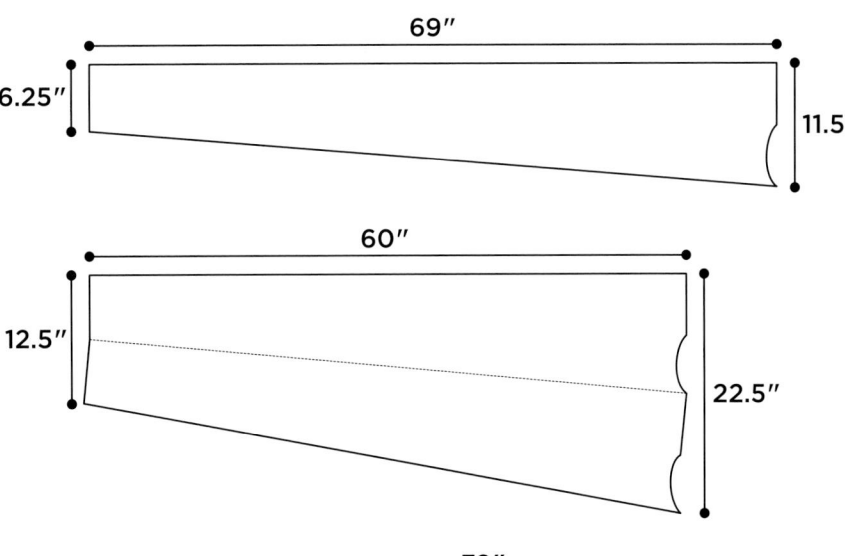
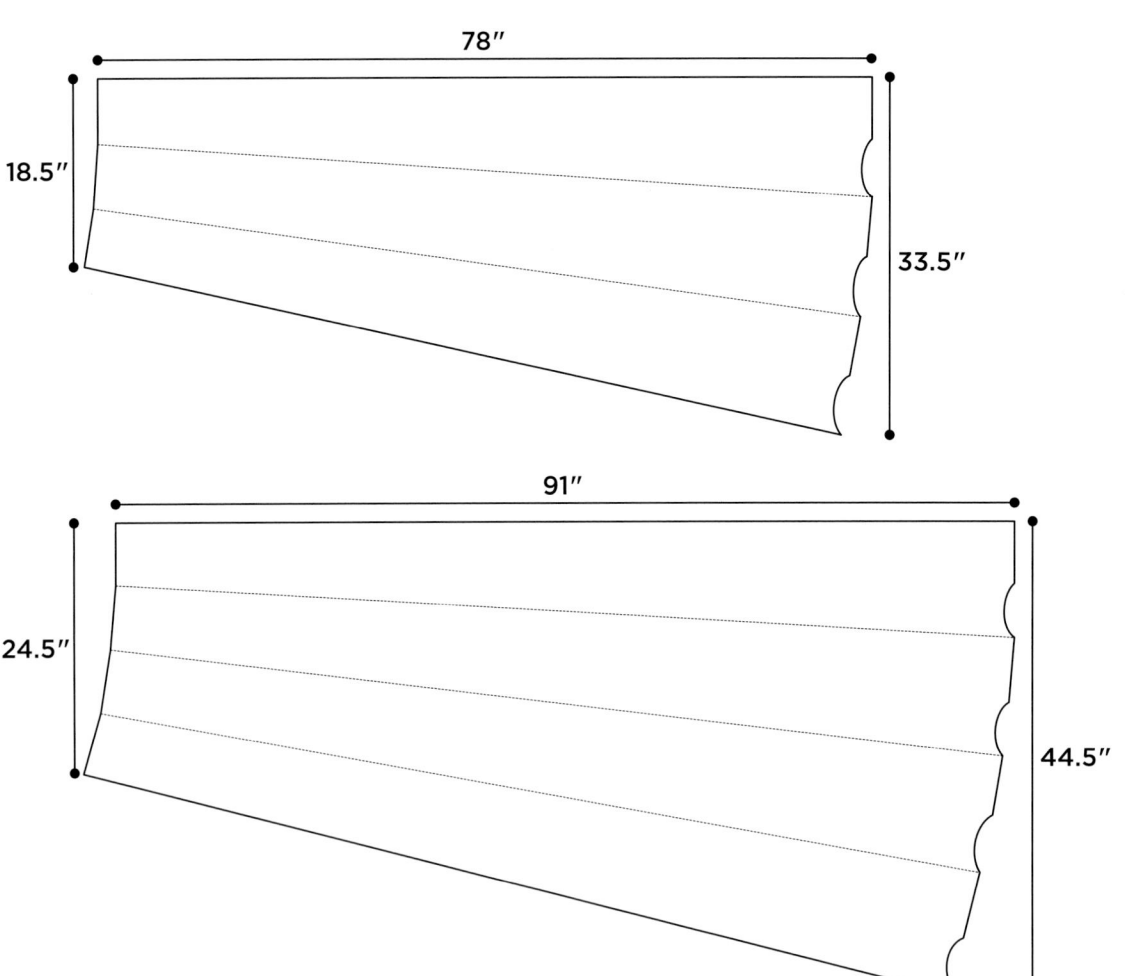

BALLINORA CARDIGAN
by Helen Metcalfe

FINISHED MEASUREMENTS
36.25 (40.25, 44.5, 48, 52)(56, 59.75, 63.75, 67.75)" finished chest circumference; meant to be worn with 8" positive ease
Sample is 40.25"; model is 34.5"

YARN
Swish™ (DK weight, 100% Fine Superwash Merino Wool; 123 yards/50g): Arctic 28639, 11 (12, 13, 14, 16)(17, 18, 19, 20) skeins

NEEDLES
US 5 (3.75mm) 24" or longer circular needles, or size to obtain gauge (while garment is worked flat, circular needles are recommended due to the large number of stitches used)

NOTIONS
Yarn Needle
Cable Needle
6 Buttons

GAUGE
24 sts and 29 rows = 4" in Twisted Rib
19 sts and 29 rows = 4" in Moss Stitch, blocked
One 33-st rep of Patchwork Cable = 4.75" wide (37 sts = 5.25" wide)
One 11-st rep of Border Pattern = 1.75" (18 sts = 3" wide)

For pattern support, contact hmetcalfe@hotmail.co.uk

Ballinora Cardigan

Notes:

Ballinora is a celebration of texture, mixing a dramatic patchwork cable with Twisted Rib and Moss Stitch. Swish gives fantastic stitch definition and is the perfect yarn for this project.

Ballinora starts with the body worked in one piece from the bottom up, then splits at the armholes where fronts and back are worked flat. Sleeves are worked flat. Short row shaping is used to shape the shawl collar.

Charts are worked flat; read RS rows (odd numbers) from right to left, and WS rows (even numbers) from left to right.

One-Row Buttonhole (worked over 3 sts)
Bring yarn to the front between needles, Sl next st P-wise and bring yarn to the back between needles, wrapping the base of the st. (Sl next st P-wise and pass first slipped st over) two times. Sl st remaining on RH needle to LH needle and turn work. With WS facing, CO 3 sts using Cable Cast On. Before placing last CO st onto LH needle, bring yarn to front between needles; place st on LH needle and turn work. Sl next st K-wise and pass last CO st over it.

2/1/2 RPC (2 over 2 Right Cable, 1 Purl center st)
Sl3 sts to CN, hold in back; K2, Sl last st from CN back to LH needle, P1, then K2 from CN.

2/2 LC (2 over 2 Left Cable)
Sl2 sts to CN, hold in front; K2, K2 from CN.

2/1 RC (2 over 1 Right Cable)
Sl1 st to CN, hold in back; K2, K1 from CN.

2/1 RPC (2 over 1 Right Cable, Purl back)
Sl1 st to CN, hold in back; K2, P1 from CN.

2/1 LPC (2 over 1 Left Cable, Purl back)
Sl2 sts to CN, hold in front; P1, K2 from CN.

2/1 LC (2 over 1 Left Cable)
Sl2 sts to CN, hold in front; K1, K2 from CN.

2/2 LPC (2 over 2 Left Cable, Purl back)
Sl2 sts to CN, hold in front; P2, K2 from CN.

2/2 RPC (2 over 2 Right Cable, Purl back)
Sl2 sts to CN, hold in back; K2, P2 from CN.

2/2 RC-PKT (2 over 2 Right Cable; P1, K1 TBL back)
Sl2 sts to CN, hold in back; K2, P1, K1 TBL from CN.

2/2 LC-KTP (2 over 2 Left Cable; K1 TBL, P1 back)
Sl2 sts to CN, hold in front; K1 TBL, P1, K2 from CN.

2/2 RC-KP-F (2 over 2 Right Cable; K1, P1 Front)
Sl2 sts to CN, hold in back; K1, P1, K2 from CN.

2/2 LC-PK (2 over 2 Left Cable; P1, K1 back)
Sl2 sts to CN, hold in front; P1, K1, K2 from CN.

Border Pattern (flat over a multiple of 11 sts plus 7)
Row 1 (RS): (P1, K1 TBL) three times, P1, *K4, (P1, K1 TBL) three times, P1; rep from * to end.
Row 2 (WS): (K1, P1 TBL) three times, K1, *P4, (K1, P1 TBL) three times, K1; rep from * to end.
Row 3: (P1, K1 TBL) three times, P1, *2/2 LC, (P1, K1 TBL) three times, P1; rep from * to end.
Row 4: Rep Row 2.
Rep Rows 1–4 for pattern.

Rope Cable (flat over 4 sts)
Row 1 (RS): K across.
Row 2 (WS): P across.
Row 3: 2/2 LC.
Row 4: P across.
Rep Rows 1–4 for pattern.

Patchwork Cable (flat over 29 sts)
Row 1 (RS): P2, K3, (P1, K1) five times, 2/1/2 RPC, P3, K2, P4.
Row 2 (WS): K4, P2, K3, P2, K1, P2, (K1, P1) five times, K1, P2, K2.
Row 3: P2, K3, (P1, K1) four times, 2/2 RC-PKT, P1, 2/2 LC-KTP, 2/1 RPC, P4.
Row 4: K5, P4, (K1, P1 TBL) twice, K1, P2, (K1, P1) four times, K1, P2, K2.
Row 5: P2, 2/1 LPC, (P1, K1) three times, 2/2 RC-PKT, (P1, K1 TBL) two times, P1, 2/2 LC, P5.
Row 6: K5, P4, (K1, P1 TBL) three times, K1, P2, (K1, P1) two times, K1, P3, K3.
Row 7: P3, 2/1 LPC, K1, P1, K1, 2/2 RC-PKT, (P1, K1 TBL) three times, P1, K4, P5.
Row 8: K5, P4, (K1, P1 TBL) four times, K1, P2, K1, P1, K1, P2, K4.
Row 9: P4, 2/1 LPC, 2/2 RC-PKT, (P1, K1 TBL) four times, P1, 2/2 LC, P5.
Row 10: K5, P4, (K1, P1 TBL) five times, K1, P4, K5.
Row 11: P5, 2/2 LC, (P1, K1 TBL) four times, P1, 2/2 RC-KP-F, 2/1 LC, P4.
Row 12: K4, P2, K1, P1, K1, P2, (K1, P1 TBL) four times, K1, P4, K5.
Row 13: P5, K4, (P1, K1 TBL) three times, P1, 2/2 RC-KP-F, K1, P1, K1, 2/1 LPC, P3.
Row 14: K3, P3, (K1, P1) two times, K1, P2, (K1, P1 TBL) three times, K1, P4, K5.
Row 15: P5, 2/2 LC, (P1, K1 TBL) two times, P1, 2/2 RC-KP-F, (K1, P1) three times, 2/1 LC, P2.
Row 16: K2, P2, (K1, P1) four times, K1, P2, (K1, P1 TBL) two times, K1, P4, K5.
Row 17: P4, 2/1 RPC, 2/2 LPC, P1, 2/2 RC-KP-F, (K1, P1) four times, K3, P2.
Row 18: K2, P2, (K1, P1) five times, (K1, P2) two times, K3, P2, K4.
Row 19: P4, K2, P3, 2/1/2 RPC, (K1, P1) five times, K3, P2.
Row 20: Rep Row 18.
Row 21: P4, 2/1 LPC, 2/2 RC-PKT, P1, 2/2 LC-KPT, (K1, P1) four times, K3, P2.
Row 22: Rep Row 16.
Row 23: P5, 2/2 LC, (P1, K1 TBL) two times, P1, 2/2 LC-KPT, (K1, P1) three times, 2/1 RPC, P2.

Row 24: Rep Row 14.
Row 25: P5, K4, (P1, K1 TBL) three times, P1, 2/2 LC-KPT, K1, P1, K1, 2/1 RPC, P3.
Row 26: Rep Row 12.
Row 27: P5, 2/2 LC, (P1, K1 TBL) four times, P1, 2/2 LC-KTP, 2/1 RPC, P4.
Row 28: Rep Row 10.
Row 29: P4, 2/1 RC, 2/2 LC-PK, (P1, K1 TBL) four times, P1, 2/2 LC, P5.
Row 30: Rep Row 8.
Row 31: P3, 2/1 RPC, K1, P1, K1, 2/2 LC-PK, (P1, K1 TBL) three times, P1, K4, P5.
Row 32: Rep Row 6.
Row 33: P2, 2/1 RC, (P1, K1) three times, 2/2 LC-PK, (P1, K1 TBL) two times, P1, 2/2 LC, P5.
Row 34: Rep Row 4.
Row 35: P2, K3, (P1, K1) four times, 2/2 LC-PK, P1, 2/2 RPC, 2/1 LPC, P4.
Row 36: Rep Row 2.
Rep Rows 1–36 for pattern.

DIRECTIONS

Body
CO 235 (259, 287, 312, 336)(365, 389, 413, 442) sts.
Rib Setup Row 1 (RS): Work Row 1 of Border Pattern from chart or written instructions, (K1 TBL, P1) 18 times, K1 TBL, P1 (1, 0, 0, 1)(0, 1, 1), (P1, K1 TBL) 4 (1, 3, 1, 1)(0, 1, 1, 0) times, work Row 1 of Border Pattern for 0 (18, 29, 29, 40)(40, 51, 62, 62) sts, (K1 TBL, P1) 53 (53, 53, 70, 70)(86, 86, 86, 103) times, K1 (1, 1, 0, 0)(1, 1, 1, 0) TBL, work Row 1 of Border Pattern for 0 (18, 29, 29, 40)(40, 51, 62, 62) sts, (K1 TBL, P1) 4 (1, 3, 1, 1)(0, 1, 1, 0) times, P1 (1, 0, 0, 1)(1, 0, 1, 1), (K1 TBL, P1) 18 times, K1 TBL, work Row 1 of Border Pattern.
Rib Setup Row 2 (WS): Work Row 2 of Border Pattern, (P1 TBL, K1) 18 times, P1 TBL, K1 (1, 0, 0, 1)(1, 0, 1, 1), (K1, P1 TBL) 4 (1, 3, 1, 1)(0, 1, 1, 0) times, work Row 2 of Border Pattern for 0 (18, 29, 29, 40)(40, 51, 62, 62) sts, (P1 TBL, K1) 53 (53, 53, 70, 70)(86, 86, 86, 103) times, P1 (1, 1, 0, 0)(1, 1, 1, 0) TBL, work Row 2 of Border Pattern for 0 (18, 29, 29, 40)(40, 51, 62, 62) sts, (P1 TBL, K1) 4 (1, 3, 1, 1)(0, 1, 1, 0) times, K1 (1, 0, 0, 1)(1, 0, 1, 1), (P1 TBL, K1) 18 times, P1 TBL, work Row 1 of Border Pattern.
Cont as established for ten more rows.

Border Pattern

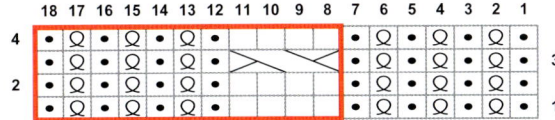

Rope Cable

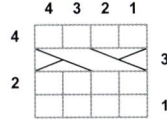

LEGEND

K
RS: Knit stitch
WS: Purl stitch

P
RS: Purl stitch
WS: Knit stitch

K TBL
RS: Knit stitch through the back loop
WS: Purl stitch through the back loop

2 over 2 Right Cable, Purl 1 center back (2/1/2 RPC)
Sl3 sts to CN, hold in back; K2, Sl last st from CN back to LH needle, P1, then K2 from CN

2 over 2 Left Cable (2/2 LC)
Sl2 to CN, hold in front; K2, K2 from CN

2 over 1 Right Cable (2/1 RC)
Sl1 to CN, hold in back; K2, K1 from CN

2 over 1 Right Cable, Purl back (2/1 RPC)
Sl1 to CN, hold in back; K2, P1 from CN

2 over 1 Left Cable, Purl back (2/1 LPC)
Sl2 to CN, hold in front; P1, K2 from CN

2 over 1 Left Cable (2/1 LC)
Sl2 to CN, hold in front; K1, K2 from CN

2 over 2 Left Cable, Purl back (2/2 LPC)
Sl2 to CN, hold in front; P2, K2 from CN

2 over 2 Right Cable, Purl back (2/2 RPC)
Sl2 to CN, hold in back; K2, P2 from CN

2 over 2 Right Cable; P1, K1 TBL back (2/2 RC-PKT)
Sl2 sts to CN, hold in back; K2, P1, K1 TBL from CN

2 over 2 Left Cable; K1 TBL, P1 back (2/2 LC-KTP)
Sl2 sts to CN, hold in front; K1 TBL, P1, K2 from CN

2 over 2 Right Cable; K1, P1 Front (2/2 RC-KP-F)
Sl2 sts to CN, hold in back; K1, P1, K2 from CN

2 over 2 Left Cable; P1, K1 back (2/2 LC-PK)
Sl2 sts to CN, hold in front; P1, K1, K2 from CN

Pattern Repeat

Row 1 (RS): Work Row 1 of Border Pattern, work Row 1 of Rope Cable, work Row 1 of Patchwork Cable, work Row 1 of Rope Cable, P1 (1, 0, 0, 1)(1, 0, 1, 1), (P1, K1 TBL) 4 (1, 3, 1, 1)(0, 1, 1, 0) times, work Row 1 of Border Pattern for 0 (18, 29, 29, 40)(40, 51, 62, 62) sts, K1 TBL, P1, Work Row 1 of Rope Cable, (work Row 1 of Patchwork Cable, work Row 1 of Rope Cable, work Row 19 of Patchwork Cable, work Row 1 of Rope Cable) 1 (1, 1, 2, 2)(2, 2, 2, 3) times, (work Row 1 of Patchwork Cable, work Row 1 of Rope Cable) 1 (1, 1, -, -)(1, 1, 1, -) time, P1, K1 TBL, work Row 1 of Border Pattern for 0 (18, 29, 29, 40)(40, 51, 62, 62) sts (K1 TBL, P1) 4 (1, 3, 1, 1)(0, 1, 1, 0) times, P1 (1, 0, 0, 1)(1, 0, 1, 1), work Row 1 of Rope Cable, work Row 19 of Patchwork Cable, work Row 1 of Rope Cable, work Row 1 of Border Pattern.

Row 2 (WS): Work Row 2 of Border Pattern, work Row 2 Rope Cable, work Row 20 of Patchwork Cable, work Row 2 of Rope Cable, K1 (1, 0, 0, 1)(1, 0, 1, 1), (K1, P1 TBL) 4 (1, 3, 1, 1) (0, 1, 1, 0) times, work Row 2 of Border Pattern for 0 (18, 29, 29, 40)(40, 51, 62, 62) sts, P1 TBL, K1, (work Row 2 of Rope Cable, work Row 2 of Patchwork Cable) 1 (1, 1, -, -)(1, 1, 1, -) time, (work Row 2 of Rope Cable, work Row 20 of Patchwork Cable, work Row 2 of Rope Cable, work Row 2 of Patchwork Cable,) 1 (1, 1, 2, 2)(2, 2, 2, 3) times, work Row 2 of Rope Cable, K1, P1 TBL, work Row 2 of Border Pattern for 0 (18, 29, 29, 40)(40, 51, 62, 62) sts, (P1 TBL, K1) 4 (1, 3, 1, 1)(0, 1, 1, 0) times, K1 (1, 0, 0, 1)(1, 0, 1, 1), work Row 2 of Rope Cable, work Row 2 of Patchwork Cable, work Row 2 of Rope Cable, work Row 2 of Border Pattern.

The last two rows set the position of patterns for duration of body. Cont to work as established until body measures 13.5 (14, 13.5, 14.75, 14.75)(14.75, 15.5, 15.5, 15.5)", ending after a WS row.

Sizes 36.25 (-, 44.5, -, -)(-, -, -, -)" Only
Next Row (RS): P1, SSK, work as established to last 3 sts, K2tog, P1. 233 (-, 285, -, -)(-, -, -, -) sts.
Next Row (WS): Work as established.
Rep last two rows once more. 231 (-, 283, -, -)(-, -, -, -) sts.

Right Front (resume all sizes)
Setup Row (RS): Work 54 (62, 67, 74, 80)(86, 92, 98, 104) sts as established, turn now working these sts only, leaving 177 (197, 216, 238, 256)(279, 297, 315, 338) sts on hold on circular needle cord.
Work 1 (1, 1, 1, 3)(7, 11, 7, 13) rows as established.
Row 1 (RS): P1, SSK, work as established to end. 1 st dec.
Row 2 (WS): Work as established.
Row 3: Rep Row 1.
Rows 4-6: Work as established.
Rep Rows 1-6 another 7 (7, 8, 8, 9)(9, 9, 10, 10) times. 38 (46, 49, 56, 60)(66, 72, 76, 82) sts.

Sizes - (40.25, -, 48, -)(-, -, -, -)" Only
Rep Rows 1-2 two more times. - (44, -, 54, -)(-, -, -, -) sts.

Resume All Sizes
Next Row (RS): Work as established.
Working as established, BO 7 (8, 9, 10, 12)(13, 14, 15, 16) sts at beginning of next 2 (1, 1, 1, 1)(4, 3, 4, 3) WS rows. 24 (36, 40, 44, 48)(14, 30, 16, 34) sts.
Working as established, BO 8 (9, 10, 11, 12)(14, 15, 16, 17) sts at beginning of next 3 (4, 4, 4, 4)(1, 2, 1, 2) WS rows. 0 sts.

Back
Slide 123 (135, 149, 164, 176)(193, 205, 217, 234) held sts to working needle, turn to work RS, now working these sts only, leaving remaining 54 (62, 67, 74, 80)(86, 92, 98, 104) sts on circular cord to hold.
WE as established until back measures 21 (21.25, 21.75, 22.75, 23.5)(24, 25.25, 25.5, 26.25)" ending after a WS row.

Shoulder Shaping
Working as established, BO 7 (8, 9, 10, 12)(13, 14, 15, 16) sts at beginning of next 4 (2, 2, 2, 2)(8, 6, 8, 6) rows. 95 (119, 131, 144, 152)(89, 121, 97, 138) sts.
Working as established, BO 8 (9, 10, 11, 12)(14, 15, 16, 17) sts at beginning of next 6 (8, 8, 8, 8)(2, 4, 2, 4) rows. 47 (47, 51, 56, 56)(61, 61, 65, 70) sts.
BO all sts.

Left Front
Slide remaining 54 (62, 67, 74, 80)(86, 92, 98, 104) sts to working needle to work RS.
Setup: Work 2 (2, 2, 2, 4)(8, 12, 8, 14) rows as established.
Row 1 (RS): Work as established to last 3 sts, K2tog, P1. 1 st dec.
Row 2 (WS): Work as established.
Row 3: Rep Row 1.
Rows 4-6: Work as established.
Rep Rows 1-6 another 7 (7, 8, 8, 9)(9, 9, 10, 10) times. 38 (46, 49, 56, 60)(66, 72, 76, 82) sts.

Sizes - (40.25, -, 48, -)(-, -, -, -)" Only
Rep Rows 1-2 two more times. - (44, -, 54, -)(-, -, -, -) sts.

Resume All Sizes
Working as established, BO 7 (8, 9, 10, 12)(13, 14, 15, 16) sts at beginning of next 2 (1, 1, 1, 1)(4, 3, 4, 3) RS rows. 24 (36, 40, 44, 48)(14, 30, 16, 34) sts.
Working as established, BO 8 (9, 10, 11, 12)(14, 15, 16, 17) sts at beginning of next 3 (4, 4, 4, 4)(1, 2, 1, 2) RS rows. 0 sts.

Sleeves (make two the same)
CO 55 (55, 55, 55, 59)(59, 59, 59, 59) sts.
Row 1 (RS): (P1, K1 TBL) 1 (1, 1, 1, 2)(2, 2, 2, 2) times, work Row 1 of Border Pattern to last 2 (2, 2, 2, 4)(4, 4, 4, 4) sts, (K1 TBL, P1) to end.
Row 2 (WS): (K1, P1 TBL) 1 (1, 1, 1, 2)(2, 2, 2, 2) times, work Row 2 of Border Pattern to last 2 (2, 2, 2, 4)(4, 4, 4, 4) sts, (P1 TBL, K1) to end.
Cont as established for ten more rows.
Selvage sts are worked in Rev St st throughout. Incorporate new sts into twisted rib pattern, increasing K or P-wise dependent on what comes next in pattern.
Inc Row: P1, M1, work as established to last st, M1, P1. 2 sts inc.
Rep Inc Row every 8 (6, 6, 6, 4)(4, 4, 4, 4) rows 5 (16, 9, 5, 23) (20, 17, 16, 11) more times. 67 (89, 75, 67, 107)(101, 95, 93, 83) sts.

Sizes 36.25 (-, 44.5, 48, -)(56, 59.75, 63.75, 67.75)" Only
Next Row: P1, M1, work as established to last st, M1, P1. 2 sts inc.
Work 5 (-, 3, 3, -)(1, 1, 1, 1) rows as established.

Rep the last 6 (-, 4, 4, -)(2, 2, 2, 2) rows 8 (-, 9, 15, -)(6, 12, 14, 24) more times. 85 (89, 95, 99, 107)(115, 121, 123, 133) sts.

Resume All Sizes
Cont as established until sleeve measures 17" or desired length, ending after a WS row.
BO all sts.

Front Bands/Collar
Sew shoulder seams using Mattress Stitch or preferred method. With RS facing, starting at lower edge of right front, PU and K 100 (101, 103, 108, 112)(114, 120, 121, 125) sts along right front, PU and K 33 (33, 35, 39, 39)(43, 43, 45, 49) sts from back neck, PU and K 100 (101, 103, 108, 112)(114, 120, 121, 125) sts along left front. 233 (235, 241, 255, 263)(271, 283, 287, 299) sts.
Row 1 (WS): (P1, K1) to last st, P1.
Rows 2-3: Rep Row 1.
Short Row 1 (RS): Work as established for 169 (171, 177, 185, 193, 201, 209, 213, 225) sts, W&T.
Short Row 2 (WS): Work as established for 105 (107, 113, 115, 123)(131, 135, 139, 151) sts, W&T.
Short Row 3: Work as established to 2 sts before previous W&T, W&T.
Rep Short Row 3 another 29 times.
Short Row 33: Work to end, closing wraps.
Next Row: Work as established, closing wraps.
Buttonhole Row: Work 5 sts as established, *work One-Row Buttonhole, work 7 (7, 7, 8, 8)(8, 9, 9, 9) sts as established; rep from * four more times, work One-Row Buttonhole, work as established to end.
Work five rows as established.
BO all sts.

Finishing
Line up center of sleeve head with shoulder seam; sew seams using Mattress Stitch. Sew sleeve seam. Rep for other sleeve. Attach buttons along left button band to line up with buttonholes.
Weave in ends, wash, and block to diagram or to achieve desired results.

Patchwork Cable

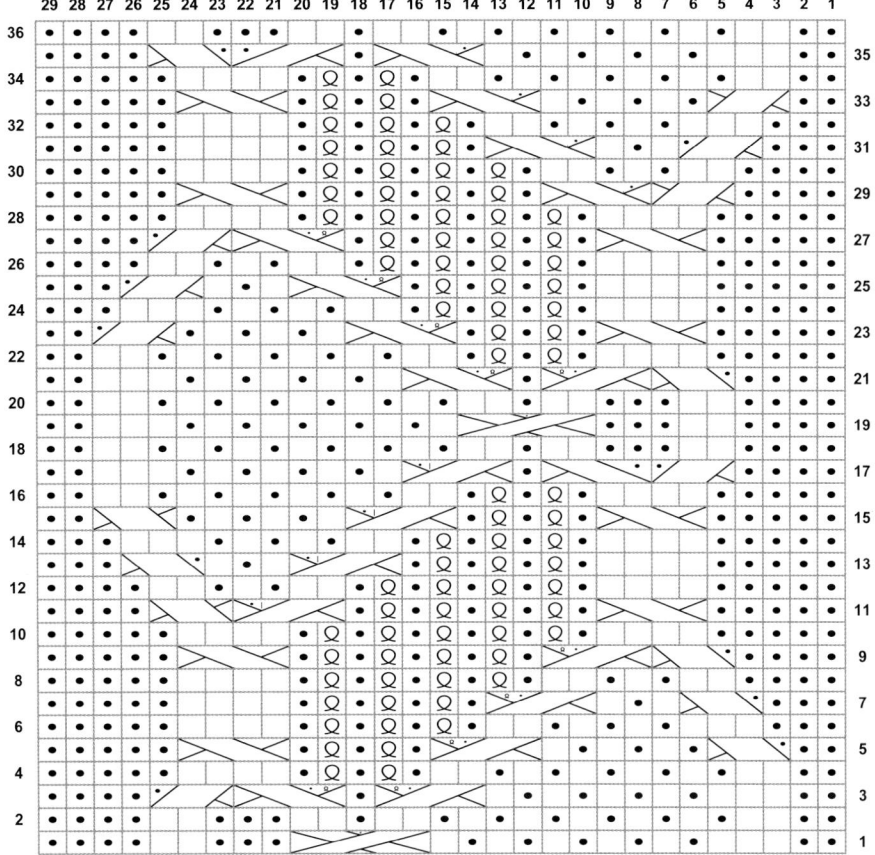

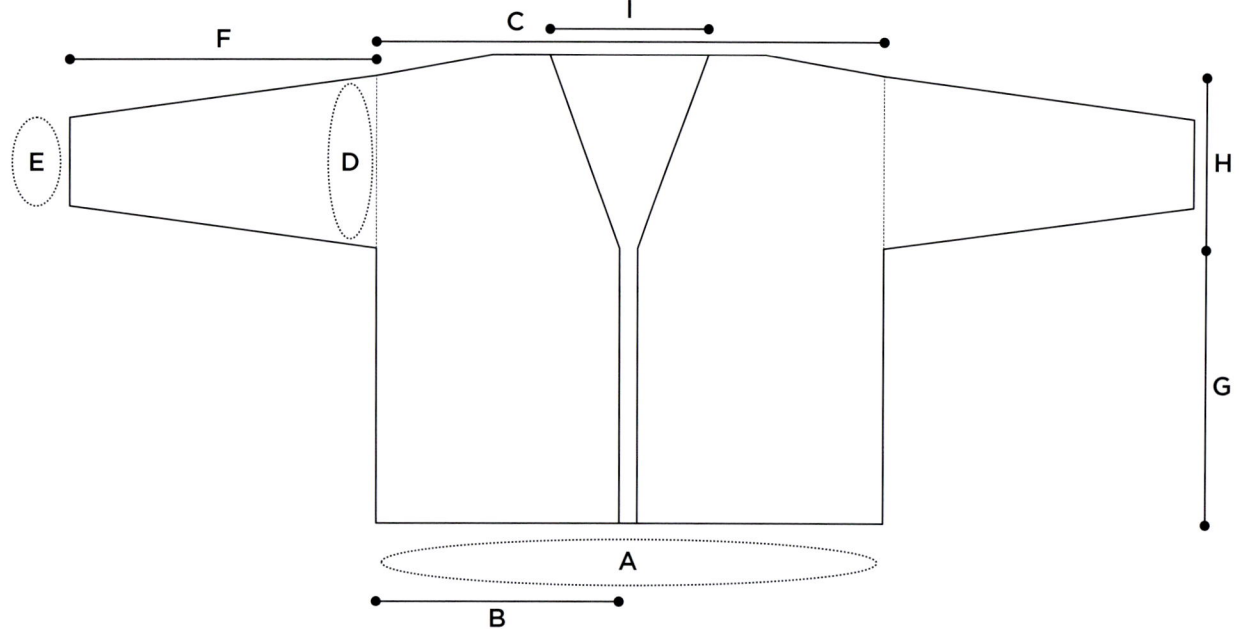

- **A** *chest circumference* 36.25 (40.25, 44.5, 48, 52)(56, 59.75, 63.75, 67.75)"
- **B** *front panel width* 8.5 (9.5, 10.25, 11.5, 12.5)(13.5, 14.5, 15.5, 16.5)"
- **C** *across back* 18 (20, 22.25, 24, 26)(28, 30, 32, 33.75)"
- **D** *upper arm circumference* 13.75 (14.5, 15.25, 16.25, 17.25)(18.5, 19.75, 20, 21.5)"
- **E** *wrist circumference* 9 (9, 9, 9, 9.5)(9.5, 9.5, 9.5, 9.5)"
- **F** *sleeve length* 17"
- **G** *length to armhole* 14 (14, 14, 14.75, 14.75)(14.75, 15.5, 15.5, 15.5)"
- **H** *length of armhole* 7 (7.25, 7.75, 8, 8.75)(9.25, 9.75, 10, 10.75)"
- **I** *back neck width* 6.75 (6.75, 7.25, 8, 8)(8.75, 8.75, 9.25, 10)"

CROSSINGS SCARF
by Mone Dräger

FINISHED MEASUREMENTS
9.5" width × 64" length

YARN
Gloss™ (DK weight, 70% Merino, 30% Silk; 123 yards/50g): Wharf 28588, 7 balls

NEEDLES
US 5 (3.75mm) straight or short circular needles, or size to obtain gauge

NOTIONS
Yarn Needle
Cable Needle
Crochet Hook for fringe (optional)

GAUGE
26 sts and 32 rows = 4" in Crossings Pattern, blocked (gauge is not crucial for the project, but will affect the finished size and amount of yarn needed)

For pattern support, contact mone.draeger@web.de

Crossings Scarf

Notes:
Cabled scarves are a timeless accessory and can be heirlooms passed down from one generation to the next. This scarf features an all-over cable pattern that forms a diamond pattern on the front and a wave-like pattern at the back resulting in two equally pretty sides.

The scarf is worked in an all-over cable pattern from one short end to the other. An I-Cord edging is maintained the entire length of the scarf. An optional fringe adds extra coziness.

Charts are worked flat; read RS rows (odd numbers) from right to left, and WS rows (even numbers) from left to right.

3/3 LC Rib (3 over 3 Left Cable, Ribbed)
Sl3 to CN, hold in front; K1, P1, K1, then K1, P1, K1 from CN.

3/3 RC Rib (3 over 3 Right Cable, Ribbed)
Sl3 to CN, hold in back; K1, P1, K1, then K1, P1, K1 from CN.

3/3 LC Purl Rib (3 over 3 Left Cable, Purl Ribbed)
Sl3 to CN, hold in front; P1, K1, P1, then P1, K1, P1 from CN.

3/3 RC Purl Rib (3 over 3 Right Cable, Purl Ribbed)
Sl3 to CN, hold in back; P1, K1, P1, then P1, K1, P1 from CN.

Crossings Pattern (flat over 64 sts)
Row 1 (RS): K1, Sl1 WYIF, K1, P2, K1, P1, K1, (K1, P1, K1, P2, K1, P1, K1) six times, K1, P1, K1, P2, K1, Sl1 WYIF, K1.
Row 2 and all WS rows: Sl1 WYIF, K1, Sl1 WYIF, K2, P1, K1, P1, (P1, K1, P1, K2, P1, K1, P1) six times, P1, K1, P1, K2, Sl1 WYIF, K1, Sl1 WYIF.
Row 3: K1, Sl1 WYIF, K1, P2, K1, P1, K1, (K1, P1, K1, P2, 3/3 RC Rib, P2, K1, P1, K1) three times, K1, P1, K1, P2, K1, Sl1 WYIF, K1.
Row 5: Rep Row 1.
Row 7: K1, Sl1 WYIF, K1, P2, K1, P1, K1, (K1, 3/3 RC Purl Rib, K2, 3/3 LC Purl Rib, K1) three times, K1, P1, K1, P2, K1, Sl1 WYIF, K1.
Row 9: Rep Row 1.
Row 11: K1, Sl1 WYIF, K1, P2, (3/3 LC Rib, P2, K1, P1, K2, P1, K1, P2) three times, 3/3 RC Rib, P2, K1, Sl1 WYIF, K1.
Row 13: Rep Row 1.
Row 15: K1, Sl1 WYIF, K1, P2, K1, P1, K1, (K1, 3/3 LC Purl Rib, K2, 3/3 Purl RC Rib, K1) three times, K1, P1, K1, P2, K1, Sl1 WYIF, K1.
Rep Rows 1–16 for pattern.

DIRECTIONS
Loosely CO 64 sts.
Work Rows 1–16 of Crossings Pattern 32 times or to desired length, from chart or written instructions.
Loosely BO all sts.

Finishing
Weave in ends, wash, and block to finished measurements or to achieve desired results.

Fringe (optional)
Cut 256 strands of yarn approx 12" long. Using a crochet hook and 2 strands of yarn, fold yarn in half, insert crochet hook into first CO st, hook folded yarn loop, and pull through st. Take ends of both yarn strands and hook them through loop made by folding the two pieces in half. Pull evenly on free ends to draw them down. Attach two strands of yarn to each st on both short ends.

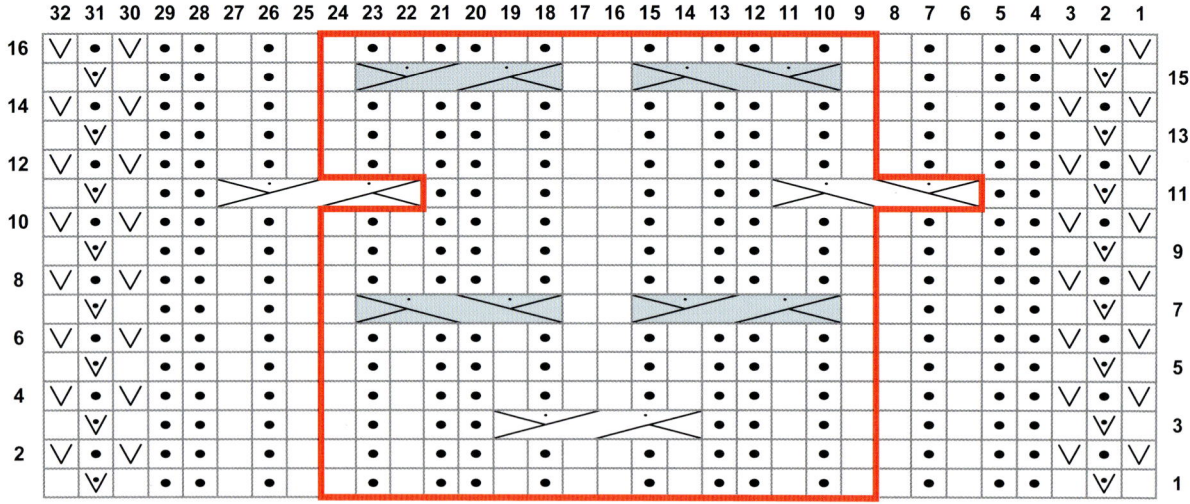

Crossings Pattern

LEGEND

K
RS: Knit stitch
WS: Purl stitch

P
RS: Purl stitch
WS: Knit stitch

Sl WYIF on WS
WS: Slip stitch purl-wise, with yarn in front

Sl WYIF on RS
RS: Slip stitch purl-wise, with yarn in front

Work boxed repeat three times

3 over 3 Left Cable, Ribbed (3/3 LC Rib)
Sl3 to CN, hold in front; K1, P1, K1, then K1, P1, K1 from CN

3 over 3 Right Cable, Ribbed (3/3 RC Rib)
Sl3 to CN, hold in back; K1, P1, K1, then K1, P1, K1 from CN

3 over 3 Left Cable, Purl Ribbed (3/3 LC Purl Rib)
Sl3 to CN, hold in front; P1, K1, P1, then P1, K1, P1 from CN

3 over 3 Right Cable, Purl Ribbed (3/3 RC Purl Rib)
Sl3 to CN, hold in back; P1, K1, P1, then P1, K1, P1 from CN

SCANDIC PULLOVER
by Donna Estin

FINISHED MEASUREMENTS
34 (38, 42, 46, 50)(54, 58, 62, 66)" finished chest circumference; meant to be worn with 4" positive ease
Sample is 38"; model is 34.5"

YARN
High Desert™ (worsted weight, 100% American Wool; 113 yards/50g): Chanterelle 29485, 15 (16, 18, 20, 22) (24, 26, 28, 29) hanks

NEEDLES
US 5 (3.5mm) 16" circular needles, or one size smaller than size used to obtain Wide Rib gauge
US 6 (4mm) 24" and 32-40" circular needles, or size to obtain gauge
US 7 (4.5mm) straight or circular needles (any length), and one set of DPNs, or size to obtain gauge

NOTIONS
Yarn Needle
Stitch Markers (at least 3 locking)
Cable Needle
Scrap Yarn

GAUGE
20 sts and 28 rnds = 4" in Reverse Stockinette Stitch with largest needles, blocked
One 22-st Chart A panel = 3" with largest needles, blocked
One 6-st Chart B panel = 1" with largest needles, blocked
20 sts and 28 rnds = 4" in Wide Rib in the round with medium sized needles, blocked (note that this is approximate due to the amount of stretch in the ribbing)

For pattern support, contact donna@donnaestin.com

Scandic Pullover

Notes:
A modern take on a cabled pullover, Scandic Pullover turns cables sideways with a gathered side to create a diagonal slant and a wide-ribbed yoke with a hint of cable funneling into a cozy turtleneck.

The body is worked flat as a large rectangle, seamed together to create the gathering on one side, and turned on its side. Sleeves are worked in the round from the bottom up. Sleeves and body come together and yoke is worked in the round in a wide rib, tapering to the turtleneck.

Charts are worked both in the round and flat. When working charts in the round, read each chart row from right to left as a RS row; when working charts flat, read RS rows (odd numbers) from right to left, and WS rows (even numbers) from left to right. Repeat lines for Chart A are only used when working sleeves.

Measure lengths vertically with weight of piece hanging from needles or by counting rows.

When working yoke, change to shorter circular needles when too few stitches remain to work comfortably.

Tubular Bind Off
Find a photo tutorial here: knitpicks.com/learning-center/tubular-bind-off.

3/3 LC (3 over 3 Left Cable)
Sl3 to CN, hold in front; K3, K3 from CN.

3/3 RC (3 over 3 Right Cable)
Sl3 to CN, hold in back; K3, K3 from CN.

2/2 LC (2 over 2 Left Cable)
Sl2 to CN, hold in front; K2, K2 from CN.

DS (Double Stitch)
Made when working German Short Rows; see *Glossary*.

Chart A (flat over 22 sts)
Row 1 (RS): (P1, K6) three times, P1.
Row 2 and all WS rows: (K1, P6) three times, K1.
Row 3: P1, K6, P1, 3/3 LC, P1, K6, P1.
Row 5: Rep Row 1.
Row 7: P1, 3/3 RC, P1, K6, P1, 3/3 RC, P1.
Row 8: Rep Row 2.
Rep Rows 1–8 for pattern.

Chart A (in the round over 22 sts)
Rnds 1–2: (P1, K6) three times, P1.
Rnd 3: P1, K6, P1, 3/3 LC, P1, K6, P1.
Rnds 4–6: Rep Rnd 1.
Rnd 7: P1, 3/3 RC, P1, K6, P1, 3/3 RC, P1.
Rnd 8: Rep Rnd 1.
Rep Rnds 1–8 for pattern.

Chart B (flat over 6 sts)
Row 1 (RS): K across.
Row 2 and all WS rows: P across.
Row 3: 3/3 LC.
Row 5: K across.
Row 7: K across.
Row 8: P across.
Rep Rows 1–8 for pattern.

Chart B (in the round over 6 sts)
Rnds 1–2: K all.
Rnd 3: 3/3 LC.
Rnds 4–8: K all.
Rep Rnds 1–8 for pattern.

DIRECTIONS

Body
With largest needles, CO 112 sts.
Setup Row (RS): P1 (selvage), (work Chart A over 22 sts, work Chart B over 6 sts, P8) two times, work Chart A over 22 sts, P1 (selvage).
Maintaining sts not in charts in Rev St st, cont to work as established until piece measures approx 34 (38, 42, 46, 50)(54, 58, 62, 66)″, ending with Row 8 of charts.
BO all sts K-wise. Break yarn, leaving a 40″ tail for seaming.

Seam CO and BO edge tog using Mattress Stitch. To create gather, with RS facing, insert yarn needle from top down between first and second st on CO edge, go under 3 full sts and bring needle up between fourth and fifth sts; rep for BO edge. Cont seaming in this manner, always going under 3 sts at a time on each side. Pull seaming yarn snugly as you go, bunching up fabric slightly, until seam measures 12″ or desired length. Be careful not to split sts so seaming yarn can move freely.
Break yarn, leaving a 6″ tail. Do not weave in ends of seaming yarn yet.

Sleeves (make two the same)
With DPNs, CO 62 (62, 62, 62)(66, 66, 66, 66) sts, distribute sts evenly on needles, PM for BOR, and join in the rnd, being careful not to twist sts.
Rnd 1: P1 (1, 1, 1)(3, 3, 3, 3), PM, work Chart A over 22 sts, P5, work Chart B over 6 sts, P5, work Chart A over 22 sts, PM, P1 (1, 1, 1)(3, 3, 3, 3).
Maintaining sts not in charts in Rev St st, cont to work as established until sleeve measures 3″.

Inc Rnd: PFB, work in pattern to last 2 sts, PFB, P1. 2 sts inc.
Cont as established and rep Inc Rnd every 11 (9, 8, 7, 6)(5, 5, 4, 4) rnds 8 (9, 11, 13, 9)(14, 6, 20, 20) more times, then every 0 (0, 0, 0, 5)(4, 4, 3, 3) rnds 0 (0, 0, 0, 8)(6, 16, 6, 6) times. 80 (82, 86, 90, 98)(108, 112, 120, 120) sts.

WE as established until sleeve measures 17 (17, 17.5, 17.5, 18)(18, 18, 18.5, 18.5)″ or desired length, ending with an odd rnd and stopping 7 (7, 8, 9, 10)(11, 11, 12, 12) sts before BOR.

Chart A

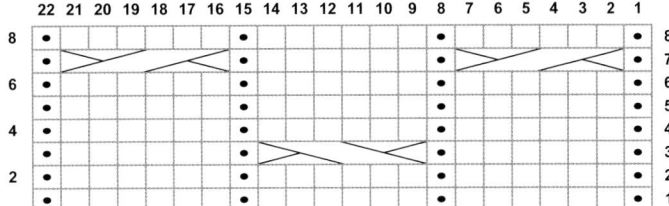

Chart B

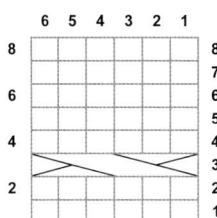

LEGEND

 Knit Stitch

• Purl Stitch

 3 over 3 Right Cable (3/3 RC)
Sl3 to CN, hold in back; K3, K3 from CN

3 over 3 Left Cable (3/3 LC)
Sl3 to CN, hold in front; K3, K3 from CN

Next Rnd: BO 14 (14, 16, 18, 20)(22, 22, 24, 24) sts, removing M when reached, P to M, remove M, (P1, K2, K2tog, K2) three times, P6, K2, K2tog, K2, P6, (K2, K2tog, K2, P1) three times, remove M, P to end. 59 (61, 63, 65, 71)(79, 83, 89, 89) sts. Place sts on scrap yarn to hold.

Fold body in half, with seam on right side. Mark center of fold with a locking M. Measure 2.75 (2.75, 3.25, 3.5, 4)(4.5, 4.5, 4.75, 4.75)" for underarm using fold M as guide for center of underarm, and PM on each end of underarm. With RS of sleeve and body facing, sew bound off sts of sleeve to body between Ms.
Rep for other underarm using seam as center of underarm. Place sleeve sts on DPNs and remove scrap yarn.

Yoke

With RS facing, and middle-sized longer circular needles, begin to the right of seam-side sleeve and *K59 (61, 63, 65, 71)(79, 83, 89, 89) sleeve sts, PM, PU and K 63 (69, 75, 89, 99)(103, 108, 120, 129) sts across body, PM; rep from * once more; join in the rnd, last M is for BOR. 244 (260, 276, 308, 340)(364, 382, 418, 436) sts.

Setup Rnd 1: *K to M, remove M, SSK, K to 2 sts before M, K2tog, remove M; rep from * once more, leaving last M in place for BOR. 240 (256, 272, 304, 336)(360, 378, 414, 432) sts.
Setup Rnd 2: *K4, P4 (4, 4, 4, 4)(5, 5, 5, 5); rep from * 29 (31, 33, 37, 41)(39, 41, 45, 47) more times.

Rnd 1: *2/2 LC, P4 (4, 4, 4, 4)(5, 5, 5, 5), K4, P4 (4, 4, 4, 4)(5, 5, 5, 5); rep from * to end.

Rnds 2-4: *K4, P4 (4, 4, 4, 4)(5, 5, 5, 5); rep from * 29 (31, 33, 37, 41)(39, 41, 45, 47) more times.
Rnd 5: *K4, P4 (4, 4, 4, 4)(5, 5, 5, 5), 2/2 LC, P4 (4, 4, 4, 4)(5, 5, 5, 5); rep from * 14 (15, 16, 18, 20)(19, 20, 22, 23) more times.
Rnds 6-8: Rep Rnds 2-4.
Rep Rnds 1-8 another 2 (2, 2, 3, 3)(3, 3, 3, 3) times, ending with Rnd 8.

Dec Rnd 1: *Sl2 to CN, hold in front, K2tog, K2 from CN, P4 (4, 4, 4, 4)(5, 5, 5, 5), K4, P4 (4, 4, 4, 4)(5, 5, 5, 5); rep from * 14 (15, 16, 18, 20)(19, 20, 22, 23) more times. 225 (240, 255, 285, 315)(340, 357, 391, 408) sts.
Next Rnd: *K3, P4 (4, 4, 4, 4)(5, 5, 5, 5), K4, P4 (4, 4, 4, 4)(5, 5, 5, 5); rep from * to end. Rep last rnd two more times.

Dec Rnd 2: *K3, P4 (4, 4, 4, 4)(5, 5, 5, 5), Sl2 to CN, hold in front, K2tog, K2 from CN, P4 (4, 4, 4, 4)(5, 5, 5, 5); rep from * 14 (15, 16, 18, 20)(19, 20, 22, 23) more times. 210 (224, 238, 266, 294)(320, 336, 368, 384) sts. (End of cables.)
Next Rnd: *K3, P4 (4, 4, 4, 4)(5, 5, 5, 5); rep from * to end. Rep last rnd four more times.

Dec Rnd 3: *K3, P1, P2tog, P1 (1, 1, 1, 1)(2, 2, 2, 2); rep from * 29 (31, 33, 37, 41)(39, 41, 45, 47) more times. 180 (192, 204, 228, 252)(280, 294, 322, 336) sts.
Next Rnd: *K3, P3 (3, 3, 3, 3)(4, 4, 4, 4); rep from * to end.

First Yoke Shaping
Begin first set of German Short Rows as follows.
Short Row 1 (RS): Work pattern as established over 46 (47, 49, 50, 55)(64, 67, 72, 72) sts, turn.
Short Row 2 (WS): Make DS, work pattern over 139 (146, 154, 167, 184)(208, 218, 237, 244) sts, turn.
Short Row 3: Make DS, work pattern to 4 sts before DS, turn.
Short Row 4: Rep Short Row 3.
Rep Short Rows 3-4 two more times.

Next Row (RS): Make DS, work pattern to BOR. End Short Rows.
Next Rnd: Work pattern to end of rnd, treating each DS as 1 st. WE in pattern for 5 (5, 7, 7, 7)(7, 7, 7, 7) more rnds.

Dec Rnd 4: *K3, P1, P2tog, P0 (0, 0, 0, 0)(1, 1, 1, 1); rep from * 29 (31, 33, 37, 41)(39, 41, 45, 47) more times. 150 (160, 170, 190, 210)(240, 252, 276, 288) sts.
Next Rnd: *K3, P2 (2, 2, 2, 2)(3, 3, 3, 3); rep from * to end. Rep last rnd 2 (4, 4, 4, 6)(6, 8, 8, 8) more times.

Dec Rnd 5: *K3, P2tog, P0 (0, 0, 0, 0)(1, 1, 1, 1); rep from * 29 (31, 33, 37, 41)(39, 41, 45, 47) more times. 120 (128, 136, 152, 168)(200, 210, 230, 240) sts.
Next Rnd: *K3, P1 (1, 1, 1, 1)(2, 2, 2, 2); rep from * to end.
Rep last rnd 0 (0, 0, 0, 0)(2, 2, 2, 4) more times.

Second Yoke Shaping
Short Row 1 (RS): Work pattern as established over 28 (30, 32, 34, 38)(48, 49, 53, 56) sts, turn.
Short Row 2 (WS): Make DS, work pattern over 92 (98, 104, 114, 126)(156, 162, 176, 184) sts, turn.
Short Row 3: Make DS, work pattern to 3 sts before DS, turn.
Short Row 4: Rep Short Row 3.
Rep Short Rows 3-4 two more times.

Next Row (RS): Make DS, work pattern to BOR. End Short Rows.
Next Rnd: Work pattern to end of rnd, treating each DS as 1 st. WE in pattern for 0 (0, 0, 0, 0)(2, 2, 2, 4) more rnds.

Sizes - (-, -, -, -)(54, 58, 62, 66)" Only
Dec Rnd 6: (K3, P2tog) to end. - (-, -, -, -)(160, 168, 184, 192) sts.
Next Rnd: (K3, P1) to end.

Resume All Sizes
Change to smallest needles and cont in K3, P1 rib for 2" or until 0.5" shorter than desired neck height.

Neckband
Rnd 1: (K1, P1) to end.
Rnd 2: (K1, Sl1 WYIF) to end. (*Note:* After slipping st, return yarn to back before knitting next st.)
Rnd 3: (Sl1 WYIB, P1) to end. (*Note:* After slipping st, bring yarn to front before purling next st.)
Rep Rnds 2-3 two more times.
BO all sts using Tubular Bind Off.

Finishing
Weave in ends, wash, and block to measurements or to achieve desired results.

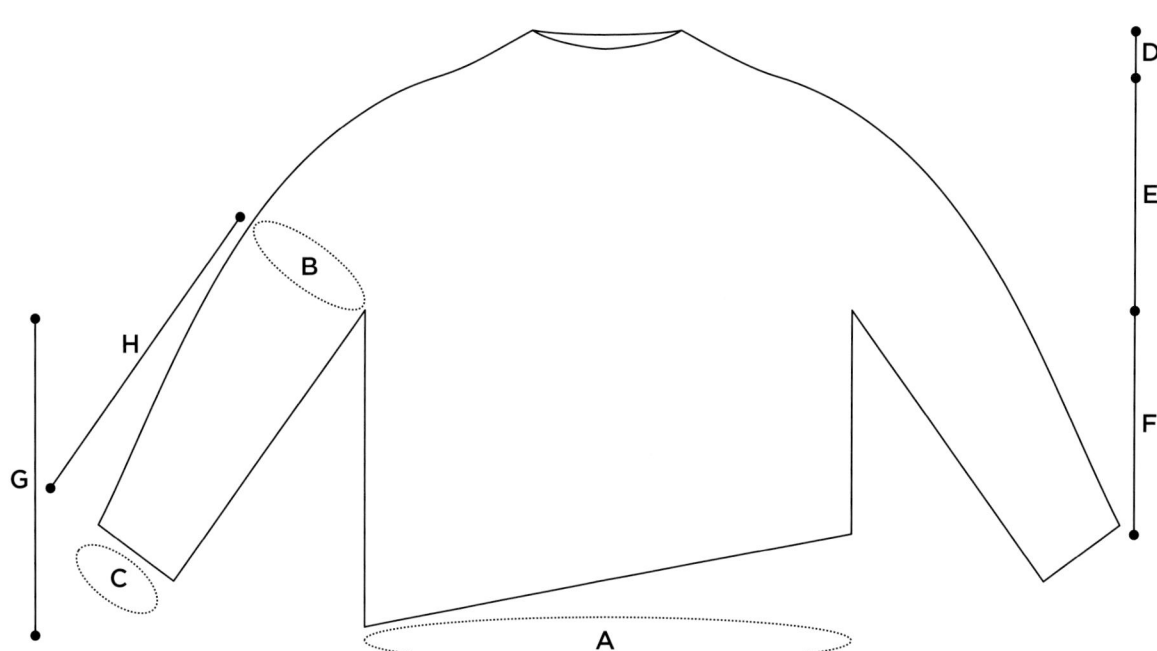

- **A** *chest circumference* 34 (38, 42, 46, 50)(54, 58, 62, 66)"
- **B** *upper arm circumference* 13 (13.5, 14.25, 15, 16.5)(18.5, 19.5, 21, 21)"
- **C** *cuff circumference* 9.5 (9.5, 9.5, 9.5, 9.5)(10.25, 10.25, 10.25, 10.25)"
- **D** *neck height* 2.5"
- **E** *yoke length* 9.5 (9.75, 10.25, 11.25, 11.5)(12.5, 12.75, 12.75, 13.25)"
- **F** *body length short side* 12"
- **G** *body length long side* 17" (or 5" longer than short side)
- **H** *sleeve length* 17 (17, 17.5, 17.5, 18)(18, 18, 18.5, 18.5)"

LYAN HAT
by Sierra Morningstar

FINISHED MEASUREMENTS
18 (19.5, 21)" circumference × 9.75" height, with brim folded over (for a traditional fitting hat, choose a size with approx 2" negative ease)

YARN
Swish™ (worsted weight, 100% Fine Superwash Merino Wool; 110 yards/50g): 2 (3, 3) skeins (yardage is for hat only; for a matching pom-pom, 18" size will need an additional skein; other two sizes will have enough yarn left over)
Size 18" sample Blossom Heather 28651
Size 19.5" sample Copper 23882

NEEDLES
US 6 (4mm) 16" circular needles and DPNs, or size to obtain gauge
US 5 (3.75mm) 16" circular needles, or one size smaller than size used to obtain gauge

NOTIONS
Yarn Needle
Stitch Marker
Waste Yarn in contrasting color
Cable Needle
Pom-Pom maker or faux fur Pom-Pom (optional)

GAUGE
32 sts and 28 rnds = 4" in Twisted Cable Pattern on larger needles, in the round and blocked
24 sts and 30 rnds = 4" in 1x1 Rib on smaller needles, blocked but not stretched (gauge is not crucial since ribbing will stretch)

For pattern support, contact Morn5420@yahoo.com

Lyan Hat

Notes:

Drawing inspiration from the constant churning of waves across the water on blustery days, the Lyan hat is adorned with a swirling cable pattern, rich in texture and movement. Its squishy fabric and cozy fit make it the perfect accessory for cold weather activities, winter beach walks included!

Lyan begins with a tubular cast on. The setup rows for the cast on are worked on larger needles, to ensure that the cast on edge is not too tight.

Chart is worked in the round; read each chart row from right to left as a RS row.

Tubular Cast On
Step 1: Using waste yarn, CO designated number of sts.
Step 2: Join working yarn. Beginning with a purl row, work four rows of St st.
Change to smaller circular needles.
Step 3: Purl first st on LH needle.
Step 4: With LH needle, pick up first st from CO edge and knit this st.
Rep Steps 3-4 until all sts have been picked up. Original number of CO sts will have doubled.
Remove waste yarn.

6/6 LPC (6 over 6 Left Cable, Purl back)
Sl6 onto CN and hold in front; P6, K6 from CN.
(Please note that the sts that were purled on the previous row will now be knit, and vice versa.)

Twisted Cable Pattern (in the round over a multiple of 12 sts)
Rnds 1-6: P6, K6.
Rnd 7: 6/6 LPC.
Rnds 8-14: P6, K6.
Rep Rnds 1-14 for pattern.

DIRECTIONS

Brim
With larger circular needles and waste yarn, CO 42 (46, 49) sts using Tubular Cast On method. 84 (92, 98) sts when CO is complete.
Remember to switch to smaller circular needles before working brim.
PM for BOR and join for working in the rnd, being careful not to twist sts.
Beginning with a purl st, work 1x1 Rib for 5".

Body
Setup Rnd: K1, (M1, K1) 18 (18, 21) times, (M1, K2) 23 (27, 27) times, (M1, K1) 18 (18, 21) times, M1, K1. 144 (156, 168) sts.
Change to larger circular needles.
Work Rnds 1-14 of Twisted Cable Pattern, repeating 12 (13, 14) times around, using chart or written instructions.
Rep full chart one more time, then rep Rnds 1-9 once more.

Crown
Switch to DPNs when necessary.
Rnd 1: (P4, P2tog, K4, K2tog) to end. 120 (130, 140) sts.
Rnd 2: (P5, K5) to end.
Rnd 3: (P3, P2tog, K3, K2tog) to end. 96 (104, 112) sts.
Rnd 4: (P4, K4) to end.
Rnd 5: (P4, K2, K2tog) to end. 84 (91, 98) sts.
Rnd 6: (P4, K3) to end.
Rnd 7: (P4, K1, K2tog) to end. 72 (78, 84) sts.
Rnd 8: (P4, K2tog) to end. 60 (65, 70) sts.
Rnd 9: (P2, P2tog, K1) to end. 48 (52, 56) sts.
Rnd 10: (P2tog, K2tog) to end. 24 (26, 28) sts.
Rnd 11: (P2tog) to end. 12 (13, 14) sts.
Rnd 12: P 0 (1, 0), (P2tog) to end. 6 (7, 7) sts.

Finishing
Break yarn, leaving a long tail. With yarn needle, pull tail through remaining 6 (7, 7) sts and pull tightly to close.
Weave in ends, wash, and block as desired.
Add optional pom-pom if desired.

Twisted Cable Pattern

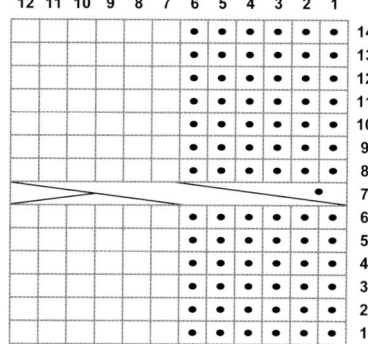

LEGEND

☐ Knit Stitch

⊡ Purl Stitch

6 over 6 Left Cable, Purl back (6/6 LPC)
Sl6 to CN, hold in front; P6, K6 from CN

ESKER WRAP
by Neisha Abdulla

FINISHED MEASUREMENTS
18" width × 78" length

YARN
Wool of the Andes™ Superwash (worsted weight, 100% Superwash Wool; 110 yards/50g): Fjord Heather 26316, 14 skeins

NEEDLES
US 6 (4mm) 24" straight or circular needles, or size to obtain gauge

NOTIONS
Yarn Needle
Cable Needle
Spare Needle for 3-Needle Bind Off
Blocking Pins and/or Wires

GAUGE
30.5 sts and 29.5 rows = 4" in Esker Pattern, blocked (gauge is not crucial, but it will affect finished size and yardage requirements)

For pattern support, contact neisha1@outlook.com

Esker Wrap

Notes:

Esker is inspired by the formation of glaciers. Carefully placed cables, irregularly shaped and often interlocking, are used to mimic the peaks and troughs typically found in glacial formations. The gender-neutral accessory will be adored by any nature-lover.

Esker is constructed in two halves and joined together using a 3-Needle Bind Off. The rib, at each end, leads gently into the cable pattern to give a seamless transition. There is a panel of moss stitch at the beginning and end of each row.

Chart is worked flat; read RS rows (odd numbers) from right to left, and WS rows (even numbers) from left to right.

3/2 RPC (3 over 2 Right Cable, Purl back)
Sl2 to CN, hold in back; K3, P2 from CN.

3/2 LPC (3 over 2 Left Cable, Purl back)
Sl3 to CN, hold in front; P2, K3 from CN.

3/3 LC (3 over 3 Left Cable)
Sl3 to CN, hold in front; K3, K3 from CN.

6/2 LPC (6 over 2 Left Cable, Purl back)
Sl6 to CN, hold in front; P2, K6 from CN.

6/2 RPC (6 over 2 Right Cable, Purl back)
Sl2 to CN, hold in back; K6, P2 from CN.

Ribbing Pattern (flat over 132 sts)
Row 1 (RS): (K1, P1) five times, K3, P6, (K4, P2, K4, P6, K6, P6) three times, K4, P2, K4, P6, K3, (P1, K1) five times.
Row 2 (WS): (K1, P1) five times, P3, K6, (P4, K2, P4, K6, P6, K6) three times, P4, K2, P4, K6, P3, (P1, K1) five times.
Rep Rows 1–2 for pattern.

Esker Pattern (worked flat over 132 sts)
Row 1 (RS): (K1, P1) five times, K3, P6, (3/2 RPC, 3/2 LPC, P6, K6, P6) three times, 3/2 RPC, 3/2 LPC, P6, K3, (P1, K1) five times.
Row 2 (WS): (K1, P1) five times, P3, K6, (P3, K4, P3, K6, P6, K6) three times, P3, K4, P3, K6, P3, (P1, K1) five times.
Row 3: (K1, P1) five times, K3, P4, (3/2 RPC, P4, 3/2 LPC, P4, K6, P4) three times, 3/2 RPC, P4, 3/2 LPC, P4, K3, (P1, K1) five times.
Row 4: (K1, P1) five times, P3, K4, (P3, K8, P3, K4, P6, K4) three times, P3, K8, P3, K4, P3, (P1, K1) five times.
Row 5: (K1, P1) five times, K3, P2, (3/2 RPC, P8, 3/2 LPC, P2, K6, P2) three times, K6, P2, 3/2 RPC, P8, 3/2 LPC, P2, K3, (P1, K1) five times.
Row 6: (K1, P1) five times, P3, (K2, P3, K12, P3, K2, P6) three times, K2, P3, K12, P3, K2, P3, (P1, K1) five times.
Row 7: (K1, P1) five times, K3, (3/2 RPC, P12, 3/2 LPC, 3/3 LC) three times, 3/2 RPC, P12, 3/2 LPC, K3, (P1, K1) five times.
Row 8: (K1, P1) five times, P6, (K16, P12) three times, K16, P6, (P1, K1) five times.
Row 9: (K1, P1) five times, (6/2 LPC, P12, 6/2 RPC) four times, (P1, K1) five times.
Row 10: (K1, P1) five times, K2, (P6, K12, P6, K4) three times, P6, K12, P6, K2, (P1, K1) five times.
Row 11: (K1, P1) five times, P2, (K6, P12, K6, P4) three times, K6, P12, K6, P2, (P1, K1) five times.
Rows 12–13: Rep Rows 10–11 once more.
Row 14: Rep Row 10.
Row 15: (K1, P1) five times, P2, (6/2 LPC, P8, 6/2 RPC, P4) three times, 6/2 LPC, P8, 6/2 RPC, P2, (P1, K1) five times.
Row 16: (K1, P1) five times, K4, (P6, K8) seven times, P6, K4, (P1, K1) five times.
Row 17: (K1, P1) five times, P4, (K6, P8) seven times, K6, P4, (P1, K1) five times.
Rows 18–19: Rep Rows 16–17 once more.
Row 20: Rep Row 16.
Row 21: (K1, P1) five times, P4, (6/2 LPC, P4, 6/2 RPC, P8) three times, 6/2 LPC, P4, 6/2 RPC, P4, (P1, K1) five times.
Row 22: (K1, P1) five times, K6, (P6, K4, P6, K12) three times, P6, K4, P6, K6, (P1, K1) five times.
Row 23: (K1, P1) five times, P6, (K6, P4, K6, P12) three times, K6, P4, K6, P6, (P1, K1) five times.
Rows 24–25: Rep Rows 22–23 once more.
Row 26: Rep Row 22.
Row 27: (K1, P1) five times, P6, (6/2 LPC, 6/2 RPC, P12) three times, 6/2 LPC, 6/2 RPC, P6, (P1, K1) five times.
Row 28: (K1, P1) five times, K8, (P12, K16) three times, P12, K8, (P1, K1) five times.
Row 29: (K1, P1) five times, P6, (3/2 RPC, K6, 3/2 LPC, P12) three times, 3/2 RPC, K6, 3/2 LPC, P6, (P1, K1) five times.
Row 30: (K1, P1) five times, K6, (P3, K2, P6, K2, P3, K12) three times, P3, K2, P6, K2, P3, K6, (P1, K1) five times.
Row 31: (K1, P1) five times, P4, (3/2 RPC, P2, K6, P2, 3/2 LPC, P8) three times, 3/2 RPC, P2, K6, P2, 3/2 LPC, P4, (P1, K1) five times.
Row 32: (K1, P1) five times, K4, (P3, K4, P6, K4, P3, K8) three times, P3, K4, P6, K4, P3, K4, (P1, K1) five times.
Row 33: (K1, P1) five times, P2, (3/2 RPC, P4, K6, P4, 3/2 LPC, P4) three times, 3/2 RPC, P4, K6, P4, 3/2 LPC, P2, (P1, K1) five times.
Row 34: (K1, P1) five times, K2, (P3, K6, P6, K6, P3, K4) three times, P3, K6, P6, K6, P3, K2, (P1, K1) five times.
Row 35: (K1, P1) five times, (3/2 RPC, P6, K6, P6, 3/2 LPC) four times, (P1, K1) five times.
Row 36: (K1, P1) five times, P3, (K8, P6) seven times, K8, P3, (P1, K1) five times.
Rep Rows 1–36 for pattern.

DIRECTIONS

First Half—Rib
CO 132 sts.
Work Rows 1–2 of Ribbing Pattern seven times.
Rep Row 1 once more.
Row 16 (WS): (K1, P1) five times, P3, K6, (P10, K6, P6, K6) three times, P10, K6, P3, (P1, K1) five times.

First Half—Body
Work Rows 1–36 of Esker Pattern, from chart or written instructions, eight times.

Place work on a spare needle until ready to join halves.

Second Half
Work the same as first half.

Join
With RSs tog, join the two halves using 3-Needle Bind Off.

Finishing
Weave in ends, wash, and block to measurements or to achieve desired results.

LEGEND

K
RS: Knit stitch
WS: Purl stitch

P
RS: Purl stitch
WS: Knit stitch

3 over 2 Right Cable, Purl back (3/2 RPC)
Sl2 to CN, hold in back; K3, P2 from CN

3 over 2 Left Cable, Purl back (3/2 LPC)
Sl3 to CN, hold in front; P2, K3 from CN

3 over 3 Left Cable (3/3 LC)
Sl3 to CN, hold in front; K3, K3 from CN

6 over 2 Right Cable, Purl back (6/2 RPC)
Sl2 to CN, hold in back; K6, P2 from CN

6 over 2 Left Cable, Purl back (6/2 LPC)
Sl6 to CN, hold in front; P2, K6 from CN

Pattern Repeat
Work three times across

Pattern Repeat
as in written pattern
(for RS rows)

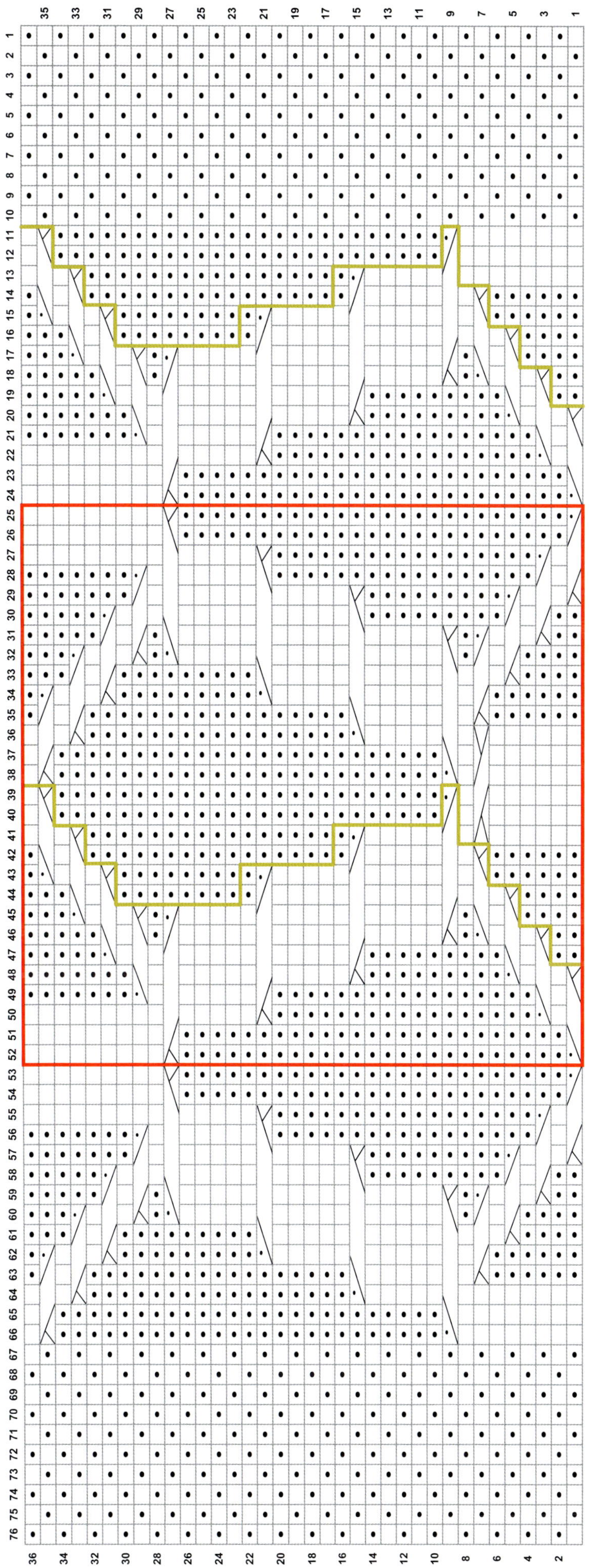

Esker Pattern

FOCUS PULLER CARDIGAN
by Holli Yeoh

FINISHED MEASUREMENTS
31 (33, 35, 37, 39)(44, 48, 51, 54)(58.25, 62, 67.75, 72, 77)" finished chest circumference, buttoned; designed to be worn with 3-5" proportional positive ease
Sample is 37"; model is 34.5"

YARN
High Desert™ (sport weight, 100% American Wool; 148 yards/50g): Woodsmoke Heather 29593, 9 (10, 11, 11, 12)(13, 15, 15, 16)(17, 19, 20, 22, 24) hanks

NEEDLES
US 4 (3.5mm) straight or circular needles (24" or longer), or size to obtain St st gauge, middle-sized needles
US 5 (3.75mm) straight or circular needles (24" or longer), or size to obtain pattern gauge, largest needles
US 3 (3.25mm) 32" circular needles, or two sizes smaller than size used to obtain pattern gauge, smallest needles

NOTIONS
Yarn Needle
Stitch Markers
Locking Stitch Markers
Cable Needle
Waste Yarn in similar weight as project yarn
Scrap Yarn or Stitch Holder
8 (8, 8, 8, 8)(7, 7, 7, 7)(7, 8, 8, 8, 8) Buttons, 0.75" diameter
Sewing Needle and Thread

GAUGE
23 sts and 34 rows = 4" in Stockinette Stitch on middle-sized needles, blocked
37 sts and 40 rows = 4" in Focus Pattern on largest needles, blocked
(you may end up using the same needle size to obtain gauge for both St st and Focus Pattern)

For pattern support, contact info@holliyeoh.com

Focus Puller Cardigan

Notes:
A dramatic rope and ring cable pattern brings fresh focus to a classic V-neck cardigan: crisp and clean, but demanding a second look. With perfect detailing in the integrated cable ribbing and lined pocket, this is a unisex modern classic.

The cardigan is worked in pieces from the bottom up and seamed together. Set-in sleeves and English-tailored shoulders provide a beautiful fit, with neat ribbed edges. Instructions are provided for working buttonholes on either the right or left side, at the knitter's discretion, with gender-inclusive language and a generous size range.

Sizing for smaller sizes is based on a 2" difference between full chest and upper chest. Upper chest is the measurement around the torso with the measuring tape at the underarm level. For sizes 48, 51, 54, 58.25, and 62 there's a 4" difference between full and upper chest. For the largest sizes there's a 6" difference between full and upper chest. In garment design, a 2/4/6" difference between full and upper chest is referred to as a B/D/F cup respectively, which differ from bra cup sizes.

When shaping in pattern, if a cable crossing cannot be completed, work the sts in St st.
Always work selvage sts in St st.

Pocket is worked as a forethought pocket. Waste yarn is placed to reserve the spot for the pocket. After Front is finished, waste yarn sts are removed and pocket lining is worked from the top edge of the opening down. Lining is then folded up and joined to the lower edge of the opening. Pocket edging is worked upwards from lower edge of opening. Side edges are seamed together.

Charts are worked flat; read RS rows (odd numbers) from right to left, and WS rows (even numbers) from left to right.

3/3 LC (3 over 3 Left Cable)
Sl3 to CN, hold in front; K3, K3 from CN.

3/3 RC (3 over 3 Right Cable)
Sl3 to CN, hold in back; K3, K3 from CN.

3/3 LPC (3 over 3 Left Cable, Purl back)
Sl3 to CN, hold in front; P3, K3 from CN.

3/3 RPC (3 over 3 Right Cable, Purl back)
Sl3 to CN, hold in back; K3, P3 from CN.

KYOK
(K1, YO, K1) all into the same stitch. 2 sts inc.

LLI (Left Lifted Increase)
Knit into the left shoulder of the stitch two below the stitch on the right-hand needle. 1 st inc.

RLI (Right Lifted Increase)
Knit into the right shoulder of the stitch one below the stitch on the left-hand needle. 1 st inc.

YO2
Double yarnover (yarn over twice). 2 sts inc.

Cabled Decreases
Double and triple decreases are worked as cable decreases, but K3tog/K4tog may be substituted for 2decB/3decB and SSSK/SSSSK may be substituted for 2decF/3decF, respectively. Of the two kinds of decreases, cabled decreases have a smooth appearance while the others are more three-dimensional. Holli has a video tutorial for cabled decreases that may be found at holliyeoh.com/tutorial/cabled-decreases.

2decB (double cabled decrease Back)
Transfer 2 sts to CN and hold at back, (K first st on LH needle tog with first st on CN) two times. 2 sts dec.

2decF (double cabled decrease Front)
Transfer 2 sts to CN and hold at front, (K first st on CN tog with first st on LH needle) two times. 2 sts dec.

3decB (triple cabled decrease Back)
Transfer 3 sts to CN and hold at back, (K first st on LH needle tog with first st on CN) three times. 3 sts dec.

3decF (triple cabled decrease Front)
Transfer 3 sts to CN and hold at front, (K first st on CN tog with first st on LH needle) three times. 3 sts dec.

Rib Setup (flat over a multiple of 27 sts, increased to 30 sts)
Row 1 (RS): P1, K3, P1, (K2, P2) two times, K2, P1, K3, P3, K3, P2.
Row 2 (WS): K2, P3, K3, P3, K1, (P2, K2) two times, P2, K1, P3, K1.
Row 3: P1, K3, P1, (K2, P2) two times, K2, P1, K3, P3, (RLI, K1) three times, P2. 30 sts.
Row 4: K2, P6, K3, P3, K1, (P2, K2) two times, P2, K1, P3, K1.

Cable Rib (flat over a multiple of 30 sts)
Row 1: P1, K3, P1, (K2, P2) two times, K2, P1, K3, P3, 3/3 LC, P2.
Row 2: K2, P6, K3, P3, K1, (P2, K2) two times, P2, K1, P3, K1.
Row 3: P1, K3, P1, (K2, P2) two times, K2, P1, K3, P3, K6, P2.
Rows 4–5: Rep Rows 2–3.
Row 6: Rep Row 2.
Rep Rows 1–6 for Cable Rib pattern.

Rib Decrease (flat over a multiple of 30 sts, decreased to 20 sts)
Row 1 (RS): P1, K3, P1, (K2, P2) two times, K2, P1, K3, P3, K6, P2.
Row 2 (WS): (K1, SSP, [P1, P2tog] two times) two times, SSP, P2tog, K1, P1, P2tog, P2, P2tog. 20 sts.

Focus Patterns
Due to the travelling nature of the cable crosses, some of the crosses in the pattern repeat shift over three sts into the adjacent chart. This happens on Rows 3, 25, and 47. This does not affect the final st count for any row.

Focus Pattern A (flat over a multiple of 30 sts, plus 6 on most rows, plus 9 on Rows 3, 25 & 47)
Transition Row 1 (RS): 3/3 LPC, (P2, K2, P2, 3/3 RPC, P3, 3/3 LC, P3, 3/3 LPC) 1 (1, 1, 2, 2)(2, 2, 3, 3)(3, 3, 4, 4, 5) time(s).

Transition Row 2 (WS): (P3, K6, P6, K6, P3, K2, P2, K2) 1 (1, 1, 2, 2)(2, 2, 3, 3)(3, 3, 4, 4, 5) time(s), P3, K3.
Transition Row 3: P3, 3/3 LPC, (3/3 RPC, P3, 3/3 RC, 3/3 LC, P3, 3/3 LPC) 1 (1, 1, 2, 2)(2, 2, 3, 3)(3, 3, 4, 4, 5) more time(s).
Transition Row 4: *(K6, P3) two times, K6, P6; rep from * 0 (0, 0, 1, 1)(1, 1, 2, 2)(2, 2, 3, 3, 4) more time(s), K6.
Row 5: P6, (3/3 LC, P3, 3/3 RC, K6, 3/3 LC, P3) 1 (1, 1, 2, 2)(2, 2, 3, 3)(3, 3, 4, 4, 5) time(s).
Row 6: (K3, P3, K12, P3, K3, P6) 1 (1, 1, 2, 2)(2, 2, 3, 3)(3, 3, 4, 4, 5) time(s), K6.
Row 7: P6, (K6, P3, K18, P3) 1 (1, 1, 2, 2)(2, 2, 3, 3)(3, 3, 4, 4, 5) time(s).
Rows 8-9: Rep Rows 6-7.
Row 10: Rep Row 6.
Row 11: P6, (3/3 LC, P3, K18, P3) 1 (1, 1, 2, 2)(2, 2, 3, 3)(3, 3, 4, 4, 5) time(s).
Rows 12-17: Rep Rows 6-11.
Rows 18-22: Rep Rows 6-10.
Row 23: P6, (3/3 LC, P3, 3/3 LPC, K6, 3/3 RPC, P3) 1 (1, 1, 2, 2)(2, 2, 3, 3)(3, 3, 4, 4, 5) time(s).
Row 24: *(K6, P3) two times, K6, P6; rep from * 0 (0, 0, 1, 1)(1, 1, 2, 2)(2, 2, 3, 3, 4) more time(s), K6.
Row 25: P3, 3/3 RC, (3/3 LC, P3, 3/3 LPC, 3/3 RPC, P3, 3/3 RC) 1 (1, 1, 2, 2)(2, 2, 3, 3)(3, 3, 4, 4, 5) time(s).
Row 26: (P3, K6, P6, K6, P3, K6) 1 (1, 1, 2, 2)(2, 2, 3, 3)(3, 3, 4, 4, 5) time(s), P3, K3.
Row 27: 3/3 RC, *K6, (3/3 LC, P3) two times, 3/3 RC; rep from * 0 (0, 0, 1, 1)(1, 1, 2, 2)(2, 2, 3, 3, 4) more time(s).
Row 28: (K3, P3, K3, P6, K3, P3, K9) 1 (1, 1, 2, 2)(2, 2, 3, 3)(3, 3, 4, 4, 5) time(s), K3, P3.
Row 29: K6, *K12, (P3, K6) two times; rep from * 0 (0, 0, 1, 1)(1, 1, 2, 2)(2, 2, 3, 3, 4) more time(s).
Rows 30-31: Rep Rows 28-29.
Row 32: Rep Row 28.
Row 33: K6, (K12, P3, 3/3 LC, P3, K6) 1 (1, 1, 2, 2)(2, 2, 3, 3)(3, 3, 4, 4, 5) time(s).
Rows 34-39: Rep Rows 28-33.
Rows 40-44: Rep Rows 28-32.
Row 45: 3/3 LPC, *K6, 3/3 RPC, P3, 3/3 LC, P3, 3/3 LPC; rep from * 0 (0, 0, 1, 1)(1, 1, 2, 2)(2, 2, 3, 3, 4) more time(s).
Row 46: *P3, K6, P6, K6, P3, K6; rep from * 0 (0, 0, 1, 1)(1, 1, 2, 2)(2, 2, 3, 3, 4) more time(s), P3, K3.
Row 47: P3, 3/3 LPC, (3/3 RPC, P3, 3/3 RC, 3/3 LC, P3, 3/3 LPC) 1 (1, 1, 2, 2)(2, 2, 3, 3)(3, 3, 4, 4, 5) time(s).
Row 48: Rep Row 24.
Rep Rows 5-48 for pattern.

Focus Pattern B (flat over 12 sts, 9 sts on Rows 3, 25 & 47)
Transition Row 1 (RS): P2, K2, P2, 3/3 RPC.
Transition Row 2 (WS): K3, P3, K2, P2, K2.
Transition Row 3: 3/3 RPC, P3.
Transition Row 4: K6, P6.
Row 5: 3/3 LC, P6.
Row 6: K6, P6.
Row 7: K6, P6.
Rows 8-9: Rep Rows 6-7.
Row 10: Rep Row 6.
Rows 11-22: Rep Rows 5-10 two times.
Rows 23-24: Rep Rows 5-6.
Row 25: 3/3 LC, P3.
Row 26: K3, P3, K6.
Row 27: K6, 3/3 LC.
Row 28: P3, K9.
Row 29: K across.
Rows 30-43: Rep Rows 28-29 seven times.
Row 44: Rep Row 28.
Row 45: K6, 3/3 RPC.
Row 46: K3, P3, K6.
Rows 47-48: Rep Rows 3-4.
Rep Rows 5-48 for pattern.

Focus Pattern C (flat over 27 sts, 24 sts on Rows 3, 25 & 47)
Transition Row 1 (RS): P2, K2, P2, 3/3 RPC, P3, 3/3 LC, P6.
Transition Row 2 (WS): K6, P6, K6, P3, K2, P2, K2.
Transition Row 3: 3/3 RPC, P3, 3/3 RC, 3/3 LC, P3.
Transition Row 4: K3, (P3, K6) two times, P6.
Row 5: 3/3 LC, P3, 3/3 RC, K6, 3/3 LC.
Row 6: P3, K12, P3, K3, P6.
Row 7: K6, P3, K18.
Rows 8-9: Rep Row 6-7.
Row 10: Rep Row 6.
Row 11: 3/3 LC, P3, K18.
Rows 12-17: Rep Rows 6-11.
Rows 18-22: Rep Rows 6-10.
Row 23: 3/3 LC, P3, 3/3 LPC, K6, 3/3 RPC.
Row 24: Rep Row 4.
Row 25: 3/3 LC, P3, 3/3 LPC, 3/3 RPC, P3.
Row 26: K6, P6, K6, P3, K6.
Row 27: K6, 3/3 LC, P3, 3/3 LC, P6.
Row 28: K6, P6, K3, P3, K9.
Row 29: K12, P3, K6, P6.
Rows 30-31: Rep Rows 28-29.
Row 32: Rep Row 28.
Row 33: K12, P3, 3/3 LC, P6.
Rows 34-39: Rep Rows 28-33.
Rows 40-44: Rep Rows 28-32.
Row 45: K6, 3/3 RPC, P3, 3/3 LC, P6.
Row 46: Rep Row 26.
Row 47-48: Rep Row 3-4.
Rep Rows 5-48 for pattern.

DIRECTIONS

Back
With smallest needles, CO 124 (132, 140, 144, 154)(174, 192, 198, 210)(228, 246, 264, 282, 302) sts.

Hem
Note: On RS rows, begin on 6th (2nd, 28th, 24th, 18th)(8th, 29th, 24th, 17th)(8th, 29th, 17th, 8th, 28th) st of Rib Setup Pattern from chart or written instructions, and end on 15th (19th, 24th, 28th, 3rd)(13th, 22nd, 28th, 4th)(13th, 22nd, 4th, 13th, 24th) st; on WS rows reverse the start and end points.
Setup Row 1 (RS): K2, P1, work Row 1 of Rib Setup to last 3 sts of row, P1, K2.

Setup Row 2 (WS): P2, K1, work Row 2 of Rib Setup to last 3 sts of row, K1, P2.
Work Rows 3-4 of Rib Setup and edge sts as established. 136 (144, 154, 162, 172)(192, 210, 222, 234)(252, 270, 294, 312, 334) sts.

Begin Cable Rib pattern as follows.
Note: On RS rows, begin on 6th (2nd, 27th, 23rd, 18th)(8th, 29th, 23rd, 17th)(8th, 29th, 17th, 8th, 27th) st of Cable Rib Pattern from chart or written instructions, and end on 15th (19th, 24th, 28th, 3rd)(13th, 22nd, 28th, 4th)(13th, 22nd, 4th, 13th, 24th) st; on WS rows reverse the start and end points.
Row 1 (RS): K2, P1, work Row 1 of Cable Rib to last 3 sts of row, P1, K2. 136 (144, 154, 162, 172)(192, 210, 222, 234)(252, 270, 294, 312, 334) sts.
Row 2 (WS): P2, K1, work Row 2 of Cable Rib Pattern to last 3 sts of row, K1, P2.
Rows 3-20: Work Cable Rib Pattern and edge sts as established.

Begin Rib Decrease pattern as follows.
Note: On RS row, begin on 6th (2nd, 27th, 23rd, 18th)(8th, 29th, 23rd, 17th)(8th, 29th, 17th, 8th, 27th) st of Rib Decrease from chart or written instructions, and end on 15th (19th, 24th, 28th, 3rd)(13th, 22nd, 28th, 4th)(13th, 22nd, 4th, 13th, 24th) st; on WS row, reverse the start and end points.
Row 1 (RS): K2, P1, work Row 1 of Rib Decrease to last 3 sts of row, P1, K2. 136 (144, 154, 162, 172)(192, 210, 222, 234)(252, 270, 294, 312, 334) sts.

Sizes 31 (-, -, 37, -)(-, -, -, 54)(-, -, 67.75, -, -)" Only
Row 2 (WS): P1, P2tog, work Rib Decrease to last 2 sts, P2. 91 (-, -, 109, -)(-, -, -, 157)(-, -, 197, -, -) sts.

Sizes - (33, -, -, -)(-, 48, 51, -)(-, 62, -, -, -)" Only
Row 2 (WS): P1, K1, SSP, work Rib Decrease to last 2 sts, P2. - (97, -, -, -)(-, 141, 149, -)(-, 181, -, -, -) sts.

Sizes - (-, 35, -, 39)(-, -, -, -)(-, -, -, -, 77)" Only
Row 2 (WS): P1, P2tog, work Rib Decrease to last 3 sts, SSP, P1. - (-, 103, -, 115)(-, -, -, -)(-, -, -, -, 223) sts.

Sizes - (-, -, -, -)(44, -, -, -)(58.25, -, -, 72, -)" Only
Row 2 (WS): P1, K1, SSP, work Rib Decrease to last 3 sts, K1, P2. - (-, -, -, -)(129, -, -, -)(169, -, -, 209, -) sts.

Resume All Sizes
Hem is 26 rows.

Body
Change to middle-sized needles.
Beginning with a RS row, WE in St st until piece measures 16.5 (16.5, 16.75, 16.5, 16.5)(15.75, 16.25, 16, 16.25)(16, 15.75, 15.75, 16, 16)" from CO edge, ending with a WS row.

Armhole Shaping
Working in St st, BO 5 (6, 7, 8, 9)(11, 13, 13, 13)(14, 14, 14, 14, 14) sts at beginning of next two rows. 81 (85, 89, 93, 97)(107, 115, 123, 131)(141, 153, 169, 181, 195) sts remain.

Sizes - (-, -, -, -)(-, 48, 51, 54)(58.25, 62, 67.75, 72, 77)" Only
Double Dec Row (RS): K2, 2decB, K to last 6 sts, 2decF, K2. 4 sts dec.
WE for one WS row.
Rep Double Dec Row every RS row - (-, -, -, -)(-, 0, 2, 3)(5, 7, 9, 11, 13) more time(s), ending with a WS row. - (-, -, -, -) (-, 111, 111, 115)(117, 121, 129, 133, 139) sts remain.

Resume All Sizes
Single Dec Row (RS): K2, K2tog, K to last 4 sts, SSK, K2. 2 sts dec.
WE for one WS row.
Rep Single Dec Row every RS row 3 (5, 6, 7, 8)(11, 10, 8, 8)(8, 8, 11, 10, 11) more times. 73 (73, 75, 77, 79)(83, 89, 93, 97)(99, 103, 105, 111, 115) sts remain.
WE until armhole measures 4.5 (5, 5.25, 5.5, 6)(6.75, 7.25, 7.25, 7.5)(7.75, 8.25, 8.25, 8.5, 9)" from underarm BO, ending with a WS row.
Place locking M through selvage sts at each end of row to indicate beginning of shoulder seam.

Shoulder Shaping
Double Dec Row (RS): K2, 2decB, K to last 6 sts, 2decF, K2. 4 sts dec.
WE for one WS row.
Rep Double Dec Row every RS row 3 (3, 4, 4, 5)(6, 8, 10, 11)(11, 11, 11, 14, 15) more times, ending with a WS row. 57 (57, 55, 57, 55)(55, 53, 49, 49)(51, 55, 57, 51, 51) sts remain.
Single Dec Row (RS): K2, K2tog, K to last 4 sts, SSK, K2. 2 sts dec.
WE for one WS row.
Rep Single Dec Row every RS row 10 (10, 9, 9, 8)(7, 5, 3, 2)(2, 4, 4, 1, 0) more time(s), ending with a WS row. 35 (35, 35, 37, 37)(39, 41, 41, 43)(45, 45, 47, 47, 49) sts remain.
BO all sts.

74 Focus Puller Cardigan

Rib Setup

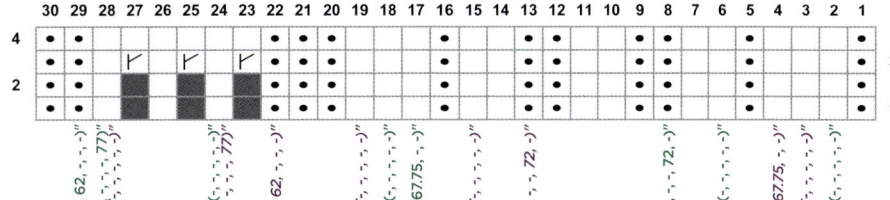

On RS rows, begin on st above green size.

On WS rows, begin on st above purple italicized size.

Cable Rib

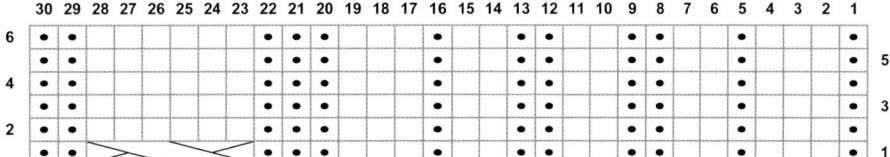

Rib Decrease

On RS rows, begin on st above green size for both Cable Rib AND Rib Decrease.

On WS rows, begin on st above purple italicized size for both Cable Rib AND Rib Decrease.

LEGEND

No Stitch
Placeholder—no stitch made

K
RS: Knit stitch
WS: Purl stitch

P
RS: Purl stitch
WS: Knit stitch

P2tog on WS
WS: Purl 2 stitches together as one stitch

SSP on WS
WS: Slip, slip, purl slipped stitches together through the back loops

RLI
Knit into the right shoulder of the stitch one below the stitch on left-hand needle

3 over 3 Right Cable (3/3 RC)
Sl3 to CN, hold in back; K3, K3 from CN

3 over 3 Left Cable (3/3 LC)
Sl3 to CN, hold in front; K3, K3 from CN

3 over 3 Right Cable, Purl back (3/3 RPC)
Sl3 to CN, hold in back; K3, P3 from CN

3 over 3 Left Cable, Purl back (3/3 LPC)
Sl3 to CN, hold in front; P3, K3 from CN

Pattern Repeat

Transition Repeat

Focus Puller Cardigan

Left Front

With smallest needles, CO 64 (68, 72, 77, 82)(91, 99, 107, 113)(120, 130, 141, 149, 161) sts.

Hem

Note: On RS rows, begin on 21st (21st, 21st, 21st, 30th)(21st, 21st, 30th, 30th)(21st, 21st, 21st, 21st, 30th) st of all Rib patterns from charts or written instructions, and end on 19th st; on WS rows reverse the start and end points.

Setup Row 1 (RS): K2, (P2, K2) 1 (2, 3, 3, 0)(1, 3, 0, 1)(1, 4, 0, 2, 0) time(s), P1 (0, 0, 3, 1)(1, 0, 0, 0)(1, 0, 0, 0), K2 (0, 0, 3, 1)(2, 0, 0, 1)(2, 0, 0, 0), P0 (1, 1, 1, 0)(0, 1, 0, 1)(0, 1, 1, 1, 0), work Row 1 of Rib Setup to last 2 (4, 4, 3, 4)(2, 4, 4, 4)(4, 4, 4, 4, 4) sts, P1 (3, 3, 2, 3)(1, 3, 3, 3)(3, 3, 3, 3, 3), K1.

Setup Row 2 (WS): P1, K1 (3, 3, 2, 3)(1, 3, 3, 3)(3, 3, 3, 3, 3), work Row 2 of Rib Setup to last 9 (11, 15, 21, 4)(9, 15, 2, 8)(9, 19, 3, 11, 2) sts, K0 (1, 1, 1, 0)(0, 1, 0, 1)(0, 1, 1, 1, 0), P2 (0, 0, 3, 1)(2, 0, 0, 1)(2, 0, 0, 0), K1 (0, 0, 3, 1)(1, 0, 0, 0)(1, 0, 0, 0), (P2, K2) 1 (2, 3, 3, 0)(1, 3, 0, 1)(1, 4, 0, 2, 0) time(s), P2. Work Rows 3–4 of Rib Setup and edge sts as established. 70 (74, 78, 83, 88)(100, 108, 116, 122)(132, 142, 156, 164, 176) sts.

Begin Cable Rib pattern as follows.

Row 1 (RS): Work first 9 (11, 15, 21, 4)(9, 15, 2, 8)(9, 19, 3, 11, 2) sts in rib as established, work Row 1 of Cable Rib to last 2 (4, 4, 3, 4)(2, 4, 4, 4)(4, 4, 4, 4, 4) sts, work remaining sts in rib as established. 70 (74, 78, 83, 88)(100, 108, 116, 122)(132, 142, 156, 164, 176) sts.

Row 2 (WS): P1, K1 (3, 3, 2, 3)(1, 3, 3, 3)(3, 3, 3, 3, 3), work Row 2 of Cable Rib to last 9 (11, 15, 21, 4)(9, 15, 2, 8)(9, 19, 3, 11, 2) sts, work remaining sts in rib as established.

Rows 3–20: Work Cable Rib and edge sts as established.

Begin Rib Decrease pattern as follows.

Row 1 (RS): Work first 9 (11, 15, 21, 4)(9, 15, 2, 8)(9, 19, 3, 11, 2) sts in rib as established, work Row 1 of Rib Decrease to last 2 (4, 4, 3, 4)(2, 4, 4, 4)(4, 4, 4, 4, 4) sts, P1 (3, 3, 2, 3)(1, 3, 3, 3)(3, 3, 3, 3, 3), K1.

Row 2 (WS): P1, K0 (2, 2, 1, 2)(0, 2, 2, 2)(2, 2, 2, 2, 2), SSP, work Row 2 of Rib Decrease to last 9 (11, 15, 21, 4)(9, 15, 2, 8)(9, 19, 3, 11, 2) sts, work remaining sts in rib as established. 49 (53, 57, 62, 61)(69, 77, 79, 85)(91, 101, 105, 113, 119) sts remain. Hem is 26 rows.

Body

Change to middle-sized needles.

Dec Row (RS): K6 (6, 3, 3, 5)(7, 6, 6, 7)(6, 8, 6, 6, 7), K2tog, *K7 (6, 5, 4, 8)(7, 6, 9, 8)(9, 5, 11, 9, 11), K2tog; rep from * 4 (5, 7, 9, 5)(6, 8, 6, 7)(7, 12, 7, 9, 8) more times, K5 (5, 3, 3, 4)(6, 5, 5, 6)(6, 7, 6, 6, 6). 44 (47, 49, 52, 55)(62, 68, 72, 77)(83, 88, 97, 103, 110) sts remain.

Purl one row.

WE in St st until piece measures 5.75 (6, 6.25, 6.25, 6.25)(6.25, 6.25, 6.5, 6.5)(6.5, 6.5, 6.5, 6.75, 6.75)" from CO edge, ending with a RS row.

Pocket Placement

P5 (6, 6, 7, 8)(10, 11, 12, 13)(15, 16, 18, 20, 22), with waste yarn P25 (25, 25, 25, 27)(27, 27, 29, 29)(29, 31, 31, 31, 31). Break waste yarn.

Transfer waste yarn sts back to LH needle.
Resume work with project yarn and P across waste yarn sts, P remaining 14 (16, 18, 20, 20)(25, 30, 31, 35)(39, 41, 48, 52, 57) sts.

WE in St st until piece measures 16.25 (16.25, 16.5, 16.25, 16.25)(15.5, 16, 15.75, 16)(15.75, 15.5, 15.5, 15.75, 15.75)" from CO edge, ending with a WS row.

Place locking M in first st of WS row (left edge when viewed from RS). M will be used when working Front Band.

Left Neck & Armhole Shaping

Armhole shaping begins on second row after initial neckline shaping row. Read through the following section before continuing.

When viewed from RS, armhole shaping is worked on right edge and neck shaping is worked on left edge.

Neck Dec Row (RS): Work to last 4 sts, SSK, K2. 1 st dec.
WE for one WS row.
Rep Neck Dec Row every RS row 9 (7, 4, 5, 3)(2, 0, 1, 4)(5, 0, 4, 3, 2) more time(s), then every four rows 6 (8, 10, 10, 12)(14, 17, 16, 15)(15, 19, 17, 18, 20) time(s).

AT THE SAME TIME, when piece measures 16.5 (16.5, 16.75, 16.5, 16.5)(15.75, 16.25, 16, 16.25)(16, 15.75, 15.75, 16, 16)" from CO edge, ending with a WS row (1 row after initial neckline shaping row), shape armhole as follows.

Armhole BO Row (RS): BO 5 (6, 7, 8, 9)(11, 13, 13, 13)(14, 14, 14, 14, 14) sts, work to end. 37 (39, 40, 42, 44)(49, 54, 57, 62)(67, 73, 81, 87, 94) sts remain.
WE for one WS row.

Sizes - (-, -, -, -)(-, 48, 51, 54)(58.25, 62, 67.75, 72, 77)" Only
Armhole Double Dec Row (RS): K2, 2decB, work to end. 2 sts dec.
WE for one WS row.
Rep Armhole Double Dec Row every RS row - (-, -, -, -)(-, 0, 2, 3)(5, 7, 9, 11, 13) more time(s), ending with a WS row.

Resume All Sizes

Armhole Single Dec Row (RS): K2, K2tog, work to end. 1 st dec.
WE for one WS row.
Rep Armhole Single Dec Row every RS row 3 (5, 6, 7, 8)(11, 10, 8, 8)(8, 8, 11, 10, 11) more times.
19 (19, 20, 20, 21)(22, 24, 26, 27)(27, 29, 29, 32, 33) sts remain when both neck and armhole shaping are complete.

WE until armhole measures 4.5 (5, 5.25, 5.5, 6)(7.25, 8.25, 8.25, 9)(9.25, 9.75, 9.75, 12.5, 13)" from Armhole BO Row, ending with a WS row.

Shoulder Shaping—Sizes 31 (33, 35, 37, 39)(44, 48, 51, 54)(58.25, 62, 67.75, -, -)" Only
Inc Row (RS): K2, RLI, work to end. 1 st inc.
WE for one WS row.
Rep Inc Row every four rows 7 (7, 7, 7, 7)(6, 5, 5, 4)(4, 4, 4, -, -) more times. 27 (27, 28, 28, 29)(29, 30, 32, 32)(32, 34, 34, -, -) sts.
WE until armhole measures 8.5 (9, 9.25, 9.5, 10)(10.75, 11.25, 11.25, 11.5)(11.75, 12.25, 12.25, -, -)", ending with a WS row.

Resume All Sizes

BO all sts.

Right Front

With smallest needles, CO 64 (68, 72, 77, 82)(91, 99, 107, 113)(120, 130, 141, 149, 161) sts.

Hem

Note: On RS rows, begin on first st of all Rib patterns from charts or written instructions and end on 30th (30th, 30th, 30th, 21st)(30th, 30th, 21st, 21st)(30th, 30th, 30th, 30th, 21st) st; on WS rows reverse the start and end points.

Setup Row 1 (RS): K1, P0 (2, 2, 1, 2)(0, 2, 2, 2)(2, 2, 2, 2, 2), work Row 1 of Rib Setup Pattern to last 9 (11, 15, 21, 4)(9, 15, 2, 8)(9, 19, 3, 11, 2) sts, P0 (1, 1, 1, 0)(0, 1, 0, 1)(0, 1, 1, 1, 0), K2 (0, 0, 3, 1)(2, 0, 0, 1)(2, 0, 0, 0, 0), P1 (0, 0, 3, 1)(1, 0, 0, 0)(1, 0, 0, 0, 0), (K2, P2) 1 (2, 3, 3, 0)(1, 3, 0, 1)(1, 4, 0, 2, 0) time(s), K2.

Setup Row 2 (WS): P2, (K2, P2) 1 (2, 3, 3, 0)(1, 3, 0, 1)(1, 4, 0, 2, 0) time(s), K1 (0, 0, 3, 1)(1, 0, 0, 0)(1, 0, 0, 0, 0), P2 (0, 0, 3, 1)(2, 0, 0, 1)(2, 0, 0, 0, 0), K0 (1, 1, 1, 0)(0, 1, 0, 1)(0, 1, 1, 1, 0), work Row 2 of Rib Setup Pattern to last 1 (3, 3, 2, 3)(1, 3, 3, 3)(3, 3, 3, 3, 3) sts, K0 (2, 2, 1, 2)(0, 2, 2, 2)(2, 2, 2, 2, 2), P1. Work Rows 3-4 of Rib Setup Pattern and edge sts as established. 70 (74, 78, 83, 88)(100, 108, 116, 122)(132, 142, 156, 164, 176) sts.

Begin Cable Rib Pattern as follows.

Row 1 (RS): K1, P0 (2, 2, 1, 2)(0, 2, 2, 2)(2, 2, 2, 2, 2), work Row 1 of Cable Rib Pattern to last 9 (11, 15, 21, 4)(9, 15, 2, 8)(9, 19, 3, 11, 2) sts, work remaining sts in rib as established.

Row 2 (WS): Work first 9 (11, 15, 21, 4)(9, 15, 2, 8)(9, 19, 3, 11, 2) sts in rib as established, work Row 2 of Cable Rib Pattern to last 1 (3, 3, 2, 3)(1, 3, 3, 3)(3, 3, 3, 3, 3) st(s), K0 (2, 2, 1, 2)(0, 2, 2, 2)(2, 2, 2, 2, 2), P1.

Rows 3-18: Work Cable Rib Pattern and edge sts as established.

Begin Focus Patterns from charts or written instructions as follows.

Transition Row 1 (RS): K1, P1 (3, 3, 2, 3)(1, 3, 3, 3)(3, 3, 3, 3, 3), work Transition Row 1 of Focus Pattern A 1 (1, 1, 2, 2)(2, 2, 2, 3, 3)(3, 3, 4, 4, 5) time(s), work Transition Row 1 of Focus Pattern C (C, C, B, B)(C, C, B, B)(C, C, B, C, B), work remaining 2 (5, 9, 2, 6)(2, 9, 3, 10)(3, 12, 13, 5, 3) sts in rib as established.

Transition Row 2 (WS): Work 2 (5, 9, 2, 6)(2, 9, 3, 10)(3, 12, 13, 5, 3) sts in rib as established, work Transition Row 2 of Focus Pattern C (C, C, B, B)(C, C, B, B)(C, C, B, C, B), work Transition Row 2 of Focus Pattern A 1 (1, 1, 2, 2)(2, 2, 3, 3)(3, 3, 4, 4, 5) time(s), work remaining 2 (4, 4, 3, 4)(2, 4, 4, 4)(4, 4, 4, 4, 4) sts in rib as established.

Work Transition Rows 3-4 as established.
Hem is 26 rows.

Body

Change to largest needles.

Row 1 (RS): K1, P1 (3, 3, 2, 3)(1, 3, 3, 3)(3, 3, 3, 3, 3), work Row 5 of Focus Pattern A 1 (1, 1, 2, 2)(2, 2, 3, 3)(3, 3, 4, 4, 5) time(s), work Row 5 of Focus Pattern C (C, C, B, B)(C, C, B, B)(C, C, B, C, B), P to last 2 sts, K2.

Row 2 (WS): P2, K0 (3, 7, 0, 4)(0, 7, 1, 8)(1, 10, 11, 3, 1), work Row 6 of Focus Pattern C (C, C, B, B)(C, C, B, B)(C, C, B, C, B), work Row 6 of Focus Pattern A 1 (1, 1, 2, 2)(2, 2, 3, 3)(3, 3, 4, 4, 5) time(s), K1 (3, 3, 2, 3)(1, 3, 3, 3)(3, 3, 3, 3, 3), P1.

Cont working patterns and edge sts as established until piece measures 16.25 (16.25, 16.5, 16.25, 16.25)(15.5, 16, 15.75, 16)(15.75, 15.5, 15.5, 15.75, 15.75)" from CO edge, ending with a WS row. Place locking M in last st worked (right edge when viewed from RS). M will be used when working Front Band.

Right Neck & Armhole Shaping

Armhole shaping begins on third row after initial neckline shaping row. Read through following section before continuing. When viewed from RS, neck shaping is worked on right edge and armhole shaping is worked on left edge. Maintain Focus Pattern throughout.

Neck Dec Row (RS): K2, K2tog, work in pattern as established to end. 1 st dec.

WS Row: Work as established to last 3 sts, P3.

Working in pattern, rep Neck Dec Row every RS row 25 (21, 20, 20, 20)(18, 14, 21, 20)(20, 21, 23, 21, 21) more time(s), then every four rows 0 (3, 4, 5, 6)(9, 13, 9, 10)(11, 12, 11, 13, 14) time(s). After neck shaping is complete, work 2 edge sts in St st to end of piece.

AT THE SAME TIME, when piece measures 16.5 (16.5, 16.75, 16.5, 16.5)(15.75, 16.25, 16, 16.25)(16, 15.75, 15.75, 16, 16)" from CO edge, ending with a RS row (2 rows after initial neckline shaping row), shape armhole as follows.

Armhole BO Row (WS): BO 5 (6, 7, 8, 9)(11, 13, 13, 13)(14, 14, 14, 14, 14) sts, work in pattern to end. 63 (66, 69, 73, 77)(87, 93, 101, 107)(116, 126, 140, 148, 160) sts remain.

Sizes - (-, -, -, -)(44, 48, 51, 54)(58.25, 62, 67.75, 72, 77)" Only

Armhole Triple Dec Row (RS): Work in pattern to last 8 sts, 3decF, K2. 3 sts dec.

WS Row: P5, work to end in pattern.

Working in pattern, rep Armhole Triple Dec Row every RS row - (-, -, -, -)(0, 1, 1, 2)(2, 3, 4, 5, 6) more time(s), ending with a WS row.

Sizes - (33, 35, 37, 39)(44, 48, 51, 54)(58.25, 62, 67.75, 72, 77)" Only

Armhole Double Dec Row (RS): Work in pattern to last 6 sts, 2decB, K2. 2 sts dec.

WS Row: P4, work to end in pattern.

Working in pattern, rep Armhole Double Dec Row every RS row - (1, 2, 3, 5)(5, 5, 8, 7)(9, 11, 12, 12, 13) more time(s), ending with a WS row.

Resume All Sizes

Armhole Single Dec Row (RS): Work in pattern to last 4 sts, SSK, K2. 1 st dec.

WS Row: P3, work to end in pattern.

Working in pattern, rep Armhole Single Dec Row every RS row 9 (8, 8, 8, 6)(9, 10, 7, 10)(11, 12, 18, 20, 24) more times.

29 (30, 31, 32, 33)(36, 38, 40, 42)(45, 45, 47, 50, 52) sts remain when both neck and armhole shaping are complete. After armhole shaping is complete, work 2 edge sts in St st to end of piece.

WE until armhole measures 8.5 (9, 9, 9.25, 9.75)(10.5, 11, 11, 11.25)(11.5, 12, 12, 12.25, 12.75)" from Armhole BO Row, ending with a WS row.

Focus Pattern A—all sizes

Note: Use smallest needles for Transition Rows 1–4, then change to largest needles.

work rep sts 1 (1, 1, 2, 2)(2, 2, 3, 3)(3, 3, 4, 4, 5) time(s)

Focus Pattern C—sizes 31 (33, 35, -, -) (44, 48, -, -)(58.25, 62, -, -)"

Focus Pattern B—sizes - (-, -, 37, 39)(-, -, 51, 54)(-, -, 67.75, -, 77)"

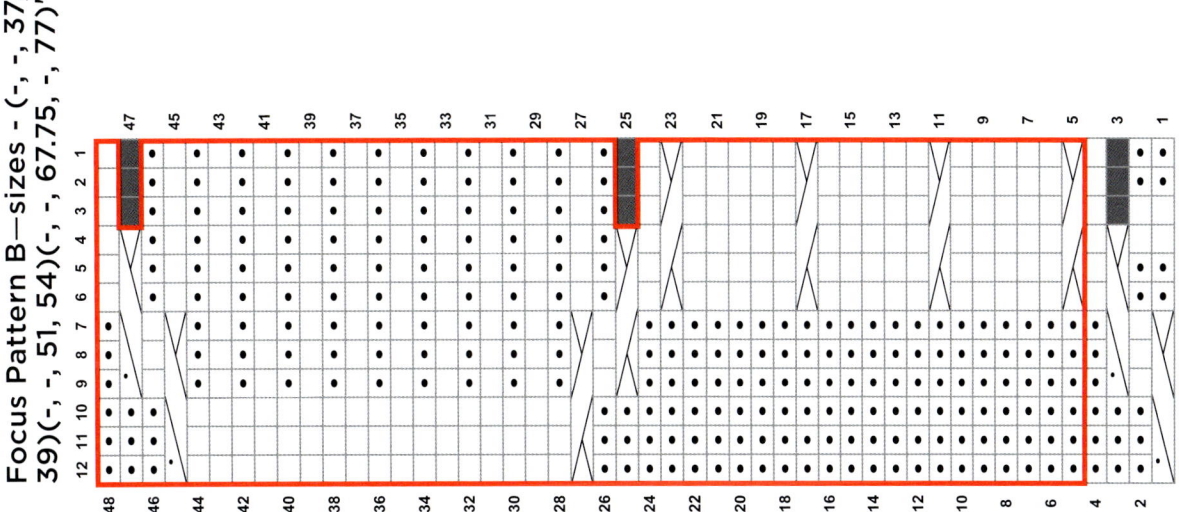

Focus Puller Cardigan 79

Shoulder Shaping—Sizes - (-, -, 37, 39)(44, 48, 51, 54)(58.25, 62, 67.75, 72, 77)" Only
Work following Dec Row in pattern as established, choosing dec technique based on the 2 sts on needle that will form the dec, as follows.
2 K sts: use K2tog.
2 P sts: use P2tog.
K st followed by P st: use SSK.
P st followed by K st: use K2tog.
Dec Row (RS): Work - (-, -, 7, 5)(2, 4, 1, 4)(1, 2, 5, 2, 8) sts, dec 1 st, *work - (-, -, 14, 9)(4, 2, 2, 1)(1, 2, 1, 1, 0) sts, dec 1 st; rep from * - (-, -, 0, 1)(4, 6, 6, 8)(11, 9, 11, 14, 16) more times, work to end. - (-, -, 30, 30)(30, 30, 30, 30)(30, 34, 34, 34, 34) sts remain.
WE for one WS row, knitting the knit sts and purling the purl sts.

Resume All Sizes
BO all sts.

Sleeves (make two the same)
Cuff
With smallest needles, CO 48 (48, 48, 48, 48)(50, 50, 50, 52)(52, 52, 56, 56, 56) sts.

Sizes 31 (33, 35, 37, 39)(-, -, -, -)(-, -, 67.75, 72, 77)" Only
Setup Row 1 (RS): K2, (P2, K2) 1 (1, 1, 1, 1)(-, -, -, -)(-, -, 2, 2, 2) time(s), PM, beginning with 20th st work Rib Setup Pattern to last 7 (7, 7, 7, 7)(-, -, -, -)(-, -, 11, 11, 11) sts, PM, P1, (K2, P2) 1 (1, 1, 1, 1)(-, -, -, -)(-, -, 2, 2, 2) time(s), K2.
Setup Row 2 (WS): P2, (K2, P2) 1 (1, 1, 1, 1)(-, -, -, -)(-, -, 2, 2, 2) time(s), K1, work Row 2 of Rib Setup Pattern to next M ending with 20th st, (P2, K2) 1 (1, 1, 1, 1)(-, -, -, -)(-, -, 2, 2, 2) time(s), P2.

Sizes - (-, -, -, -)(44, 48, 51, 54)(58.25, 62, -, -, -)" Only
Setup Row 1 (RS): K2, P- (-, -, -, -)(2, 2, 2, 3)(3, 3, -, -, -), K3, PM, beginning with 20th st work Rib Setup Pattern to last 7 (7, 7, 7, 7)(8, 8, 8, 9)(9, 9, 11, 11, 11) sts, PM, P1, K3, P- (-, -, -, -)(2, 2, 2, 3)(3, 3, -, -, -), K2.
Setup Row 2 (WS): P2, K- (-, -, -, -)(2, 2, 2, 3)(3, 3, -, -, -), P3, K1, beginning with 30th st work Row 2 of Rib Setup Pattern to next M, P3, K- (-, -, -, -)(2, 2, 2, 3)(3, 3, -, -, -), P2.

Resume All Sizes
Work Rows 3-4 of Rib Setup Pattern and edge sts as established. 54 (54, 54, 54, 54)(56, 56, 56, 58)(58, 58, 62, 62, 62) sts.

Begin Cable Rib Pattern as follows.
Row 1 (RS): Work to M in rib as established, beginning with 20th st work Cable Rib Pattern to next M, work to end in rib as established.
Row 2 (WS): Work to M in rib as established, work Row 2 of Cable Rib Pattern to next M ending with 20th st, work to end in rib as established.
Rows 3-27: Work Cable Rib Pattern and edge sts as established, ending with a RS row.
Dec Row (WS): Removing Ms as they are reached, work to M in pattern, K1, SSP, (P1, P2tog) two times, work in pattern to 10 sts before next M, K1, SSP, (P1, P2tog) two times, work in pattern to end. 48 (48, 48, 48, 48)(50, 50, 50, 52)(52, 52, 56, 56, 56) sts. Cuff is 32 rows.

Sleeve Shaping
Change to middle-sized needles.
Beginning with a K row, work two rows in St st.
Inc Row (RS): K2, RLI, K to last 2 sts, LLI, K2. 2 sts inc.
WE for one WS row.
Working in St st, rep Inc Row every 10 (10, 8, 6, 6)(4, 4, 4, 2)(2, 2, 2, 2, 2) rows 1 (7, 8, 1, 5)(1, 22, 26, 2)(8, 14, 18, 24, 30) more time(s). 52 (64, 66, 52, 60)(54, 96, 104, 58)(70, 82, 94, 106, 118) sts.
Then rep Inc Row every 12 (12, 10, 8, 8)(6, 6, 0, 4)(4, 4, 4, 4, 4) rows 7 (2, 3, 11, 8)(16, 2, 0, 25)(22, 20, 19, 16, 14) time(s). 66 (68, 72, 74, 76)(86, 100, 104, 108)(114, 122, 132, 138, 146) sts.
WE until sleeve measures 17.5 (17.5, 17.5, 17.5, 17.5)(18, 18, 18.5, 18.5)(18.5, 19, 19.5, 19.5, 20)" from CO edge, ending with a WS row.

Sleeve Cap Shaping
BO 5 (6, 7, 8, 9)(11, 13, 13, 13)(14, 14, 14, 14, 14) sts at beginning of next two rows. 56 (56, 58, 58, 58)(64, 74, 78, 82)(86, 94, 104, 110, 118) sts remain.

Sizes - (-, -, -, -)(-, -, -, -)(-, -, 67.75, 72, 77)" Only
Double Dec Row (RS): K2, 2decB, K to last 6 sts, 2decF, K2. 4 sts dec.
WE for one WS row.
Rep Double Dec Row every RS row - (-, -, -, -)(-, -, -, -)(-, -, 2, 4, 6) more times, ending with a WS row. - (-, -, -, -)(-, -, -, -)(-, -, 92, 90, 90) sts remain.

Resume All Sizes
Single Dec Row (RS): K2, K2tog, K to last 4 sts, SSK, K2. 2 sts dec.
WE for one WS row.
Rep Single Dec Row every RS row 11 (8, 9, 8, 5)(8, 17, 19, 22)(24, 26, 27, 26, 26) more times, ending with a WS row. 32 (38, 38, 40, 46)(46, 38, 38, 36)(36, 40, 36, 36, 36) sts remain.
Then rep Single Dec Row every 4 (4, 4, 4, 4)(4, 4, 4, 4)(4, 4, -, -, -) rows 1 (4, 4, 5, 8)(8, 4, 3, 2)(2, 2, -, -, -) times time(s), ending with a WS row. 30 (30, 30, 30, 30)(30, 30, 32, 32)(32, 36, 36, 36, 36) sts remain.
Double Dec Row (RS): K2, 2decB, K to last 6 sts, 2decF, K2. 4 sts dec.
WE for one WS row.
Rep Double Dec Row two more times, ending with a WS row. 18 (18, 18, 18, 18)(18, 18, 20, 20)(20, 24, 24, 24, 24) sts remain.
BO all sts.

Finishing
Wash and gently block pieces to schematic measurements. Stretch out shoulder BO edge of cabled right front to match schematic measurement, if needed. Left front has been shaped for sizes 31–67.75" to accommodate the longer shoulder edge and does not require stretching.

Pocket
Pocket Opening
With RS of left front facing, place 25 (25, 25, 25, 27)(27, 27, 29, 29)(29, 31, 31, 31, 31) sts from row directly below waste yarn sts onto scrap yarn or st holder.

With smallest needles, place 25 (25, 25, 25, 27)(27, 27, 29, 29)(29, 31, 31, 31, 31) sts from row directly above waste yarn sts onto needle. Remove waste yarn.

Pocket Lining
Change to middle-sized needles.
Inc Row (RS): With RS facing, join yarn and K1, LLI, K to last st, RLI, K1. 27 (27, 27, 27, 29)(29, 29, 31, 31)(31, 33, 33, 33, 33) sts. Beginning with a P row, work St st until lining measures 6.5 (7, 7.5, 7.5, 7.5)(7.5, 7.5, 8, 8)(8, 8, 8, 8.5, 8.5)" from Inc Row, ending with a RS row.

Transfer sts from lower edge of pocket opening to smallest needle.
Fold lining in half with RS tog, tuck folded lining through opening so lining is on WS but sts on needle remain on RS. With RS facing, hold needles parallel to one another with pocket opening sts in front of pocket lining sts.
Joining Row (RS): Using an empty smallest needle and using working yarn attached to back (pocket lining) needle, K1 on back needle, *insert needle K-wise into next st on front needle and next st on back needle and K both sts tog; rep from * to last st on back needle, K1. 27 (27, 27, 27, 29)(29, 29, 31, 31)(31, 33, 33, 33, 33) sts.

Pocket Edging
Row 1 (WS): P2, (K1, P1) to last st, P1.
Row 2 (RS): K2, (P1, K1) to last st, K1.
Rep Rows 1-2 two more times, then Row 1 once more.
BO in pattern.

Pocket Seaming
Using Mattress Stitch, sew sides of edging to cardigan front. Sew side seams of pocket lining tog.
If desired, tack down lower corners of pocket to inside of cardigan to secure pocket bottom.

Front Band
Join Shoulders: Join left front shoulder to left back shoulder from M to neckline BO. Rep for right shoulder. Remove shoulder seam Ms.

With RS facing and smallest needles, PU and K 105 (105, 107, 105, 105)(101, 105, 103, 105)(103, 101, 101, 103, 103) sts along right front opening from hem to M, remove M and place on needle, cont to PU and K: 62 (64, 66, 68, 70)(74, 80, 80, 82)(84, 90, 90, 92, 96) sts to right shoulder seam, 33 (33, 33, 35, 35)(37, 39, 39, 41)(43, 43, 45, 45, 47) sts across back neckline, 62 (64, 66, 68, 70)(74, 80, 80, 82)(84, 90, 90, 92, 96) sts along left front neckline to M; remove M and place on needle, PU and K 105 (105, 107, 105, 105)(101, 105, 103, 105)(103, 101, 101, 103, 103) sts to CO edge of hem. 367 (371, 379, 381, 385)(387, 409, 405, 415)(417, 425, 427, 435, 445) sts.
Row 1 (WS): (P1, K1) to last st, PFB. 368 (372, 380, 382, 386)(388, 410, 406, 416)(418, 426, 428, 436, 446) sts.
Row 2 (RS): K1, (K1, P1) to last st, KFB. 369 (373, 381, 383, 387)(389, 411, 407, 417)(419, 427, 429, 437, 447) sts.
1x1 Rib is established with 2 St st selvage sts at each end of row. Maintain pattern throughout Front Band.
Row 3: Work as established to M, SM, KYOK, work to 1 st before next M, KYOK, work to end. 373 (377, 385, 387, 391)(393, 415, 411, 421)(423, 431, 433, 441, 451) sts.

Buttonholes may be placed on either right or left side of front opening for what's traditionally considered a women's or men's closure (respectively).
Choose whichever side is more comfortable for you or for the intended recipient of the cardigan.
Next, proceed to either Right or Left Front Buttonhole Row.
Right Front Buttonhole Row 4 (RS): Work 6 (6, 8, 6, 6)(4, 6, 6, 6)(6, 4, 4, 6, 6) sts as established, K2tog, YO2, *work 12 (12, 12, 12, 12)(14, 12, 14, 12)(14, 14, 14, 14, 14) sts, K2tog, YO2; rep from * 6 (6, 6, 6, 6)(5, 6, 5, 6)(5, 5, 5, 5, 5) more times, work to end. 8 (8, 8, 8, 8)(7, 8, 7, 8)(7, 7, 7, 7, 7) buttonholes.
Left Front Buttonhole Row 4 (RS): Work to second M as established, K1, YO2, K2tog, *work 12 (12, 12, 12, 12)(14, 12, 14, 12)(14, 14, 14, 14, 14) sts, YO2, K2tog; rep from * 6 (6, 6, 6, 6)(5, 6, 5, 6)(5, 5, 5, 5, 5) more times, work to end. 8 (8, 8, 8, 8)(7, 8, 7, 8)(7, 7, 7, 7, 7) buttonholes.

Resume All Buttonhole Placement Options
Row 5: *Work as established to YO2, Sl1 WYIF letting second wrap from YO2 fall off needle; rep from * for all YO2, work to end.
Row 6: *Work to Sl st, WYIF insert RH needle from back to front under float from Sl st AND through YO and P both strands tog; rep from * for all buttonholes, work to end.
Row 7: Rep Row 3. 377 (381, 389, 391, 395)(397, 419, 415, 425)(427, 435, 437, 445, 455) sts.
Rows 8-9: Work as established to end.
BO all sts in pattern.

Final Finishing
PMs on armhole edge of left and right fronts 2" (approx 17 rows on left front and 20 rows on right front) below shoulder seam. Set in sleeves, matching center of sleeve cap with M on front. Using Mattress Stitch, sew sleeve and side seams.
Weave in ends.
Sew on buttons to correspond with buttonholes.

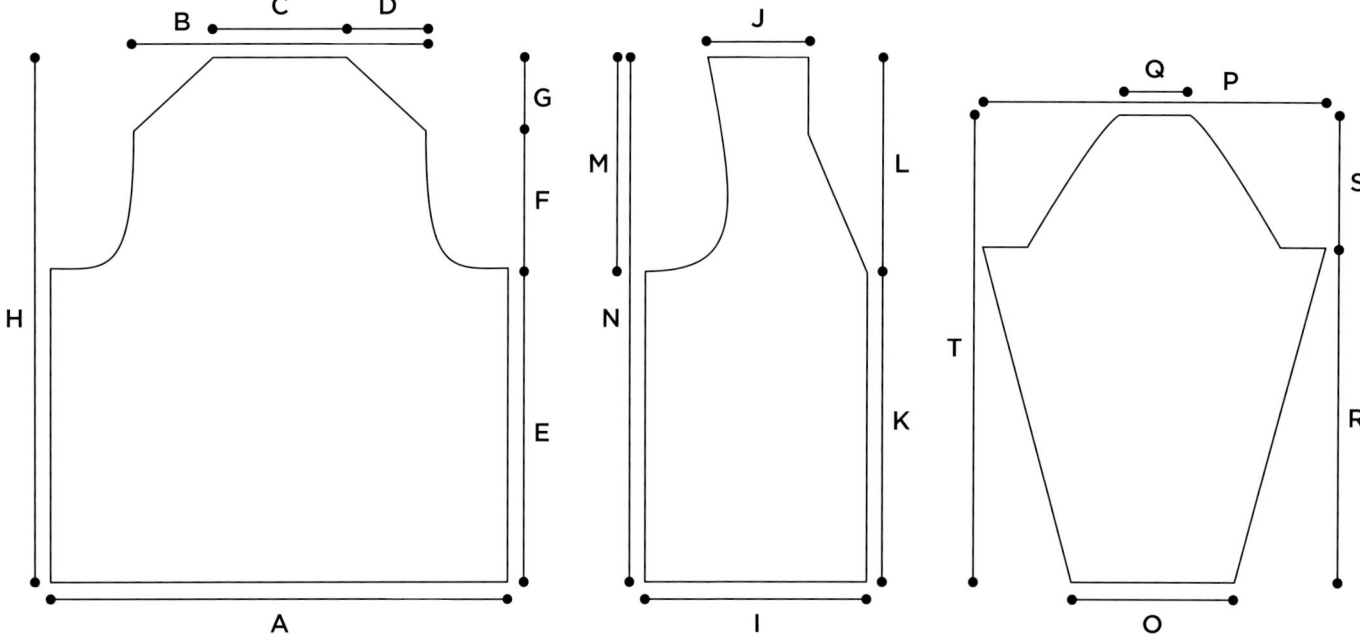

A *body width* 15.75 (16.75, 18, 19, 20)(22.5, 24.5, 26, 27.25)(29.5, 31.5, 34.25, 36.25, 38.75)"
B *upper back width* 12.75 (12.75, 13, 13.5, 13.75)(14.5, 15.5, 16.25, 16.75)(17.25, 18, 18.25, 19.25, 20)"
C *back neck width* 6 (6, 6, 6.5, 6.5)(6.75, 7.25, 7.25, 7.5)(7.75, 7.75, 8.25, 8.25, 8.5)"
D *back shoulder width* 3.25 (3.25, 3.5, 3.5, 3.75)(3.75, 4.25, 4.5, 4.75)(4.75, 5, 5, 5.5, 5.75)"
E *body length to underarm* 16.5 (16.5, 16.75, 16.5, 16.5)(15.75, 16.25, 16, 16.25)(16, 15.75, 15.75, 16, 16)"
F *back armhole depth* 4.5 (5, 5.25, 5.5, 6)(6.75, 7.25, 7.25, 7.5)(7.75, 8.25, 8.25, 8.5, 9)"
G *back shoulder drop* 3.5 (3.5, 3.5, 3.5, 3.5)(3.5, 3.5, 3.75, 3.75)(3.75, 4, 4, 4, 4)"
H *total back length* 24.75 (25.25, 25.75, 25.75, 26.25)(26.25, 27.25, 27, 27.5)(27.5, 28, 28, 28.5, 29)"
I *one side of cardigan width* 7.75 (8.25, 8.5, 9, 9.5)(10.75, 11.75, 12.5, 13.5)(14.5, 15.25, 16.75, 18, 19.25)"
J *front shoulder width* 4.75 (4.75, 4.75, 4.75, 5)(5, 5.25, 5.5, 5.5)(5.5, 6, 6, 5.5, 5.75)"
K *front opening length* 16.25 (16.25, 16.5, 16.25, 16.25)(15.5, 16, 15.75, 16)(15.75, 15.5, 15.5, 15.75, 15.75)"
L *front neck drop* 8.75 (9.25, 9.5, 9.75, 10.25)(11, 11.5, 11.5, 11.75)(12, 12.5, 12.5, 12.75, 13.25)"
M *front armhole depth* 8.5 (9, 9.25, 9.5, 10)(10.75, 11.25, 11.25, 11.5)(11.75, 12.25, 12.25, 12.5, 13)"
N *total front length* 25 (25.5, 26, 26, 26.5)(26.5, 27.5, 27.25, 27.75)(27.75, 28, 28, 28.5, 29)"
O *unseamed wrist width* 8.25 (8.25, 8.25, 8.25, 8.25)(8.75, 8.75, 8.75, 9)(9, 9, 9.75, 9.75, 9.75)"
P *unseamed full sleeve width* 11.5 (11.75, 12.5, 12.75, 13.25)(15, 17.5, 18, 18.75)(19.75, 21.25, 23, 24, 25.5)"
Q *top of sleeve cap width* 3.25 (3.25, 3.25, 3.25, 3.25)(3.25, 3.25, 3.5, 3.5)(3.5, 4.25, 4.25, 4.25, 4.25)"
R *sleeve seam length* 17.5 (17.5, 17.5, 17.5, 17.5)(18, 18, 18.5, 18.5)(18.5, 19, 19.5, 19.5, 20)"
S *sleeve cap depth* 4.25 (5, 5.25, 5.5, 6)(6.75, 7, 7, 7.25)(7.75, 8.25, 8.25, 8.5, 9)"
T *total sleeve length* 21.75 (22.5, 22.75, 23, 23.5)(24.75, 25, 25.5, 25.75)(26.25, 27.25, 27.75, 28, 29)"

KNOTS SHAWL
by Mone Dräger

FINISHED MEASUREMENTS
65.5" wingspan × 44" height

YARN
Wool of the Andes™ (sport weight, 100% Peruvian Highland Wool; 137 yards/50g): Papaya Heather 25301, 9 skeins

NEEDLES
US 4 (3.5mm) 32" or longer circular needles, or size to obtain gauge

NOTIONS
Yarn Needle
Cable Needle

GAUGE
20 sts and 32 rows = 4" in cable patterns, blocked (gauge is not crucial, but it will affect finished size and yardage requirements)

For pattern support, contact mone.draeger@web.de

Knots Shawl

Notes:
During the summer months, the neighbor's chain-linked fence is overgrown with Indian cress and very popular with the butterflies. This pattern was inspired by this sight. It uses an all-over cable pattern to form diamond-shaped segments, filled with small butterfly-shaped insertions.

The triangle-shaped shawl starts at the bottom tip and is knit from the bottom up. All increases are made in pattern. The side edges are I-Cords worked with the shawl; the top edge is an I-Cord knit on sideways to end the shawl.

Charts are worked flat; read RS rows (odd numbers) from right to left, and WS rows (even numbers) from left to right.

M1P (Make 1 P-wise)
Inserting LH needle from back to front, PU the horizontal strand before the next st, and purl.

LT (1 over 1 Left Twist)
Sl1 to CN, hold in front; K1, K1 from CN.

RT (1 over 1 Right Twist)
Sl1 to CN, hold in back; K1, K1 from CN.

2/2 LC (2 over 2 Left Cable)
Sl2 to CN, hold in front; K2, K2 from CN.

2/2 RC (2 over 2 Right Cable)
Sl2 to CN, hold in back; K2, K2 from CN.

2/1 LC (2 over 1 Left Cable)
Sl2 to CN, hold in front; K1, K2 from CN.

2/1 RC (2 over 1 Right Cable)
Sl1 to CN, hold in back; K2, K1 from CN.

2/1 LPC (2 over 1 Left Cable, Purl Back)
Sl2 to CN, hold in front; P1, K2 from CN.

2/1 RPC (2 over 1 Right Cable, Purl Back)
Sl1 to CN, hold in back; K2, P1 from CN.

Setup Pattern (flat over an increasing st count)
Row 1 (RS): KFB, K1, KFB. 5 sts.
Row 2 (WS): P across.
Row 3: KFB, K2, KFB, K1. 7 sts.
Row 4: (Sl1 WYIF, K1) three times, Sl1 WYIF.
Row 5: K1, Sl1 WYIF, K1, M1P, P1, K1, Sl1 WYIF, K1. 8 sts.
Row 6: Sl1 WYIF, K1, Sl1 WYIF, K2, Sl1 WYIF, K1, Sl1 WYIF.
Row 7: K1, Sl1 WYIF, K1, M1P, K2, M1P, K1, Sl1 WYIF, K1. 10 sts.
Row 8: (Sl1 WYIF, K1) two times, P2, (K1, Sl1 WYIF) two times.
Row 9: K1, Sl1 WYIF, K1, M1P, K4, M1P, K1, Sl1 WYIF, K1. 12 sts.
Row 10: (Sl1 WYIF, K1) two times, P4, (K1, Sl1 WYIF) two times.
Row 11: K1, Sl1 WYIF, K1, M1P, 2/1 RPC, 2/1 LPC, M1P, K1, Sl1 WYIF, K1. 14 sts.
Row 12: (Sl1 WYIF, K1) two times, P2, K2, P2, (K1, Sl1 WYIF) two times.
Row 13: K1, Sl1 WYIF, K1, M1P, P1, K2, P2, K2, P1, M1P, K1, Sl1 WYIF, K1. 16 sts.
Row 14: Sl1 WYIF, K1, Sl1 WYIF, (K2, P2) two times, K2, Sl1 WYIF, K1, Sl1 WYIF.
Row 15: K1, Sl1 WYIF, K1, M1P, P1, 2/1 RPC, P2, 2/1 LPC, P1, M1P, K1, Sl1 WYIF, K1. 18 sts.
Row 16: Sl1 WYIF, K1, Sl1 WYIF, K2, P2, K4, P2, K2, Sl1 WYIF, K1, Sl1 WYIF.
Row 17: K1, Sl1 WYIF, K1, M1P, P1, 2/1 RPC, P4, 2/1 LPC, P1, M1P, K1, Sl1 WYIF, K1. 20 sts.
Row 18: Sl1 WYIF, K1, Sl1 WYIF, K2, P2, K6, P2, K2, Sl1 WYIF, K1, Sl1 WYIF.
Row 19: K1, Sl1 WYIF, K1, M1P, P1, 2/1 RPC, P2, K2, P2, 2/1 LPC, P1, M1P, K1, Sl1 WYIF, K1. 22 sts.
Row 20: Sl1 WYIF, K1, Sl1 WYIF, K2, (P2, K3) two times, P2, K2, Sl1 WYIF, K1, Sl1 WYIF.
Row 21: K1, Sl1 WYIF, K1, M1P, P1, 2/1 RPC, P2, K4, P2, 2/1 LPC, P1, M1P, K1, Sl1 WYIF, K1. 24 sts.
Row 22: Sl1 WYIF, K1, Sl1 WYIF, K2, P2, K3, P4, K3, P2, K2, Sl1 WYIF, K1, Sl1 WYIF.
Row 23: K1, Sl1 WYIF, K1, M1P, P1, 2/1 RPC, P2, K6, P2, 2/1 LPC, P1, M1P, K1, Sl1 WYIF, K1. 26 sts.
Row 24: Sl1 WYIF, K1, Sl1 WYIF, K2, P2, K3, P6, K3, P2, K2, Sl1 WYIF, K1, Sl1 WYIF.
Row 25: K1, Sl1 WYIF, K1, M1P, P1, 2/1 RPC, P2, K8, P2, 2/1 LPC, P1, M1P, K1, Sl1 WYIF, K1. 28 sts.
Row 26: Sl1 WYIF, K1, Sl1 WYIF, K2, P2, K3, P8, K3, P2, K2, Sl1 WYIF, K1, Sl1 WYIF.
Row 27: K1, Sl1 WYIF, K1, M1P, P1, 2/1 RPC, P3, 2/2 LC, 2/2 RC, P3, 2/1 LPC, P1, M1P, K1, Sl1 WYIF, K1. 30 sts.
Row 28: Sl1 WYIF, K1, Sl1 WYIF, K2, P2, K4, P8, K4, P2, K2, Sl1 WYIF, K1, Sl1 WYIF.
Row 29: K1, Sl1 WYIF, K1, M1P, P1, 2/1 RC, P4, K8, P4, 2/1 LC, P1, M1P, K1, Sl1 WYIF, K1. 32 sts.
Row 30: Sl1 WYIF, K1, Sl1 WYIF, K2, P3, K4, P8, K4, P3, K2, Sl1 WYIF, K1, Sl1 WYIF.
Row 31: K1, Sl1 WYIF, K1, M1P, P1, 2/1 RPC, LT, P3, 2/2 RC, 2/2 LC, P3, RT, 2/1 LPC, P1, M1P, K1, Sl1 WYIF, K1. 34 sts.
Row 32: Sl1 WYIF, K1, Sl1 WYIF, K2, P2, K1, P2, K3, P8, K3, P2, K1, P2, K2, Sl1 WYIF, K1, Sl1 WYIF.
Row 33: K1, Sl1 WYIF, K1, M1P, P1, 2/1 RC, P1, 2/1 LPC, P3, K6, P3, 2/1 RPC, P1, 2/1 LC, P1, M1P, K1, Sl1 WYIF, K1. 36 sts.
Row 34: Sl1 WYIF, K1, Sl1 WYIF, K2, P3, K2, P2, K3, P6, K3, P2, K2, P3, K2, Sl1 WYIF, K1, Sl1 WYIF.
Row 35: K1, Sl1 WYIF, K1, M1P, P1, 2/1 RPC, LT, P1, 2/1 LPC, P3, K4, P3, 2/1 RPC, P1, RT, 2/1 LPC, P1, M1P, K1, Sl1 WYIF, K1. 38 sts.
Row 36: Sl1 WYIF, K1, Sl1 WYIF, K2, P2, K1, P2, K2, P2, K3, P4, K3, P2, P2, K1, P2, K2, Sl1 WYIF, K1, Sl1 WYIF.

Main Pattern (flat over an increasing st count)
Row 1 (RS): K1, Sl1 WYIF, K1, P2, K2, P1, (2/1 LPC, P1, 2/1 LPC, P3, K2, P3, 2/1 RPC, P1, 2/1 RPC) to last 8 sts, P1, K2, P2, K1, Sl1 WYIF, K1.
Row 2 (WS): Sl1 WYIF, K1, Sl1 WYIF, K2, P2, K1, *K1, P2, K2, (P2, K3) two times, P2, K2, P2, K1; rep from * to last 8 sts, K1, P2, K2, Sl1 WYIF, K1, Sl1 WYIF.

Row 3: K1, Sl1 WYIF, K1, M1P, P1, 2/1 RPC, P1, *(P1, 2/1 LPC) two times, P6, (2/1 RPC, P1) two times; rep from * to last 8 sts, P1, 2/1 LPC, P1, M1P, K1, Sl1 WYIF, K1. 2 sts inc.
Row 4: Sl1 WYIF, K1, Sl1 WYIF, K2, P2, K2, *(K2, P2) two times, K6, (P2, K2) two times; rep from * to last 9 sts, K2, P2, K2, Sl1 WYIF, K1, Sl1 WYIF.
Row 5: K1, Sl1 WYIF, K1, M1P, P1, 2/1 RPC, P2, (P2, 2/1 LPC, P1, 2/1 LPC, P4, 2/1 RPC, P1, 2/1 RPC, P2) to last 9 sts, P2, 2/1 LPC, P1, M1P, K1, Sl1 WYIF, K1. 2 sts inc.
Row 6: Sl1 WYIF, K1, Sl1 WYIF, K2, P2, K3, (K3, P2, K2, P2, K4, P2, K2, P2, K3) to last 10 sts, K3, P2, K2, Sl1 WYIF, K1, Sl1 WYIF.
Row 7: K1, Sl1 WYIF, K1, M1P, P1, 2/1 RPC, P2, K1, (K1, P2, 2/1 LPC, P1, 2/1 LPC, P2, 2/1 RPC, P1, 2/1 RPC, P2, K1) to last 10 sts, K1, P2, 2/1 LPC, P1, M1P, K1, Sl1 WYIF, K1. 2 sts inc.
Row 8: Sl1 WYIF, K1, Sl1 WYIF, K2, P2, K3, P1, *P1, K3, (P2, K2) three times, P2, K3, P1; rep from * to last 11 sts, P1, K3, P2, K2, Sl1 WYIF, K1, Sl1 WYIF.
Row 9: K1, Sl1 WYIF, K1, M1P, P1, 2/1 RPC, P2, K2, (K2, P2, 2/1 LPC, P1, 2/1 LPC, 2/1 RPC, P1, 2/1 RPC, P2, K2) to last 11 sts, K2, P2, 2/1 LPC, P1, M1P, K1, Sl1 WYIF, K1. 2 sts inc.
Row 10: Sl1 WYIF, K1, Sl1 WYIF, K2, P2, K2, P3, (P3, K2, P2, K2, P4, K2, P2, K3, P2) to last 12 sts, P2, K3, P2, K2, Sl1 WYIF, K1, Sl1 WYIF.
Row 11: K1, Sl1 WYIF, K1, M1P, P1, 2/1 RPC, P2, K3, (K3, P2, 2/1 LPC, P1, K4, P1, 2/1 RPC, P2, K3) to last 12 sts, K3, P2, 2/1 LPC, P1, M1P, K1, Sl1 WYIF, K1. 2 sts inc.
Row 12: Sl1 WYIF, K1, Sl1 WYIF, K2, P2, K3, P3, (P3, K3, P2, K1, P4, K1, P2, K3, P3) to last 13 sts, P3, K3, P2, K2, Sl1 WYIF, K1, Sl1 WYIF.
Row 13: K1, Sl1 WYIF, K1, M1P, P1, 2/1 RPC, P2, K4, (K4, P2, 2/1 LPC, 2/2 LC, 2/1 RPC, P2, K4) to last 13 sts, K4, P2, 2/1 LPC, P1, M1P, K1, Sl1 WYIF, K1. 2 sts inc.
Row 14: Sl1 WYIF, K1, Sl1 WYIF, K2, P2, K3, P4, (P4, K3, P8, K3, P4) to last 14 sts, P4, K3, P2, K2, Sl1 WYIF, K1, Sl1 WYIF.
Row 15: K1, Sl1 WYIF, K1, M1P, P1, 2/1 RPC, P3, 2/2 LC, (2/2 RC, P3, K8, P3, 2/2 LC) to last 14 sts, 2/2 RC, P3, 2/1 LPC, P1, M1P, K1, Sl1 WYIF, K1. 2 sts inc.
Row 16: Sl1 WYIF, K1, Sl1 WYIF, K2, P2, K4, P4, (P4, K3, P8, K3, P4) to last 15 sts, P4, K4, P2, K2, Sl1 WYIF, K1, Sl1 WYIF.
Row 17: K1, Sl1 WYIF, K1, M1P, P1, 2/1 RC, P4, K4, (K4, P3, 2/2 RC twice, P3, K4) to last 15 sts, K4, P4, 2/1 LC, P1, M1P, K1, Sl1 WYIF, K1. 2 sts inc.
Row 18: Sl1 WYIF, K1, Sl1 WYIF, K2, P3, K4, P4, (P4, K3, P8, K3, P4) to last 16 sts, P4, K4, P3, K2, Sl1 WYIF, K1, Sl1 WYIF.
Row 19: K1, Sl1 WYIF, K1, M1P, P1, 2/1 RPC, LT, P3, 2/2 RC, (2/2 LC, P3, K8, P3, 2/2 RC) to last 16 sts, 2/2 LC, P3, RT, 2/1 LPC, P1, M1P, K1, Sl1 WYIF, K1. 2 sts inc.
Row 20: Sl1 WYIF, K1, Sl1 WYIF, K2, P2, K1, P2, K3, P4, (P4, K3, P8, K3, P4) to last 17 sts, P4, K3, P2, K1, P2, K2, Sl1 WYIF, K1, Sl1 WYIF.
Row 21: K1, Sl1 WYIF, K1, M1P, P1, 2/1 RC, P1, 2/1 LPC, P3, K3, (K3, P3, 2/1 RPC, 2/2 LC, 2/1 LPC, P3, K3) to last 17 sts, K3, P3, 2/1 RPC, P1, 2/1 LC, P1, M1P, K1, Sl1 WYIF, K1. 2 sts inc.
Row 22: Sl1 WYIF, K1, Sl1 WYIF, K2, P3, K2, P2, K3, P3, (P3, K3, P2, K1, P4, K1, P2, K3, P3) to last 18 sts, P3, K3, P2, K2, P3, K2, Sl1 WYIF, K1, Sl1 WYIF.
Row 23: K1, Sl1 WYIF, K1, M1P, P1, 2/1 RPC, LT, K1, 2/1 LPC, P3, K2, (K2, P3, 2/1 RPC twice, 2/1 LPC twice, P3, K2) to last 18 sts, K2, P3, 2/1 RPC, P1, RT, 2/1 LPC, P1, M1P, K1, Sl1 WYIF, K1. 2 sts inc.
Row 24: Sl1 WYIF, K1, Sl1 WYIF, K2, P2, K1, P2, K2, P2, K3, P2, (P2, K3, P2, K1, P2, K2, P2, K1, P2, K3, P2) to last 19 sts, P2, K3, P2, K1, P3, K1, P2, K2, Sl1 WYIF, K1, Sl1 WYIF.
Rep Rows 1–24 for pattern.

Top Pattern (flat over an increasing st count)
Row 1 (RS): K1, Sl1 WYIF, K1, M1P, P1, 2/1 RPC, P4, K4, (K4, P3, 2/2 RC two times, P3, K4) 13 times, K4, P4, 2/1 LPC, P1, M1P, K1, Sl1 WYIF, K1. 318 sts.
Row 2 (WS): Sl1 WYIF, K1, Sl1 WYIF, K2, P2, K5, P4, (P4, K3, P8, K3, P4) 13 times, P4, K5, P2, K2, Sl1 WYIF, K1, Sl1 WYIF.
Row 3: K1, Sl1 WYIF, K1, M1P, P1, 2/1 RPC, P5, 2/2 RC, (2/2 LC, P3, K8, P3, 2/2 RC) 13 times, 2/2 LC, P5, 2/1 LPC, P1, M1P, K1, Sl1 WYIF, K1. 320 sts.
Row 4: Sl1 WYIF, K1, Sl1 WYIF, K2, P2, K6, P4, (P4, K3, P8, K3, P4), P4, K6, P2, K2, Sl1 WYIF, K1, Sl1 WYIF.
Row 5: K1, Sl1 WYIF, K1, M1P, P1, 2/1 RPC, P7, K3, (K3, P4, K2, 2/2 LC, K2, P4, K3) 13 times, K3, P7, 2/1 LPC, P1, M1P, K1, Sl1 WYIF, K1. 322 sts.
Row 6: Sl1 WYIF, K1, Sl1 WYIF, K2, P2, K8, P3, (P3, K4, P8, K4, P3), P3, K8, P2, K2, Sl1 WYIF, K1, Sl1 WYIF.
Row 7: K1, Sl1 WYIF, K1, M1P, P1, 2/1 RPC, P9, K2, (K2, P5, K8, P5, K2) 13 times, K2, P9, 2/1 LPC, P1, M1P, K1, Sl1 WYIF, K1. 324 sts.
Row 8: Sl1 WYIF, K1, Sl1 WYIF, K2, P2, K10, P2, (P2, K5, P8, K5, P2) 13 times, P2, K10, P2, K2, Sl1 WYIF, K1, Sl1 WYIF.
Row 9: K1, Sl1 WYIF, K1, M1P, P1, 2/1 RPC, P11, K1, (K1, P6, 2/2 RC twice, P6, K1) 13 times, K1, P11, 2/1 LPC, P1, M1P, K1, Sl1 WYIF, K1. 326 sts.
Row 10: Sl1 WYIF, K1, Sl1 WYIF, K2, P2, K12, P1, (P1, K6, P8, K6, P1) 13 times, P1, K12, P2, K2, Sl1 WYIF, K1, Sl1 WYIF.
Row 11: K1, Sl1 WYIF, K1, M1P, P1, 2/1 RPC, P13, (P7, K2, 2/2 LC, K2, P7) 13 times, P13, 2/1 LPC, P1, M1P, K1, Sl1 WYIF, K1. 328 sts.
Row 12: Sl1 WYIF, K1, Sl1 WYIF, K2, P2, K14, (K7, P8, K7) 13 times, K14, P2, K2, Sl1 WYIF, K1, Sl1 WYIF.

DIRECTIONS

Body
CO 3 sts.
Work Rows 1–36 of Setup Pattern, from chart or written instructions. 38 sts.
Work Rows 1–24 of Main Pattern twelve times, then rep Rows 1–16 once more. 316 sts.
Work Rows 1–12 of Top Pattern. 328 sts.

Top Edge
The top edge is an I-Cord knit on sideways along the body sts. Beginning with Row 4, the third st of the I-Cord is worked tog with the first body st.
Row 1: K3, return all sts to LH needle.
Rows 2–3: Rep Row 1.
Row 4: K2, SSK, return all sts to LH needle. 1 body st BO.
Rep Row 4 until 3 body sts remain.
Next Row: K3, return all sts to LH needle.
Rep last row two more times.

Knots Shawl

Break yarn and graft I-Cord sts tog with remaining body sts.

Finishing
Weave in ends, wash, and block to measurements or to achieve desired results.

A *width* 65.5"
B *height* 44"

Setup Pattern

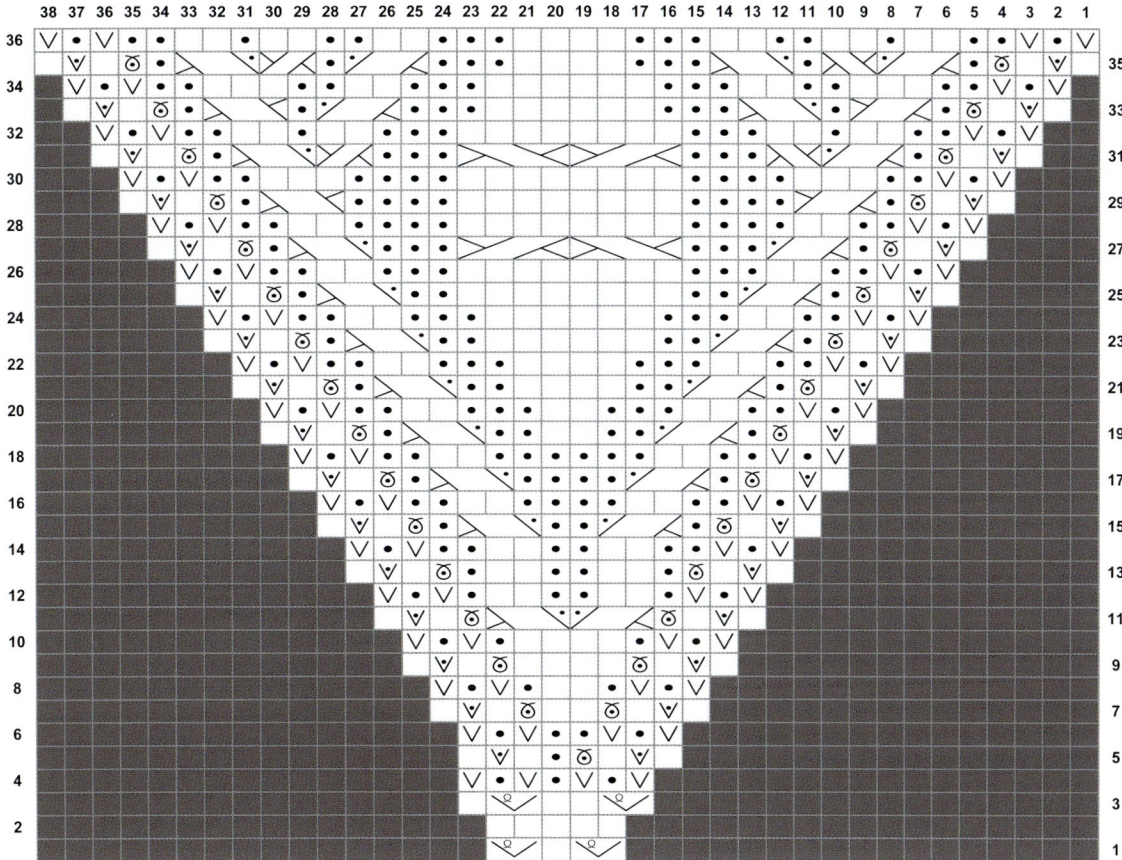

LEGEND

- ■ **No Stitch** — Placeholder—no stitch made
- □ **K** — RS: Knit stitch / WS: Purl stitch
- • **P** — RS: Purl stitch / WS: Knit stitch
- ⱽ **Sl WYIF on RS** — RS: Slip stitch purl-wise, with yarn in front
- V **Sl WYIF on WS** — WS: Slip stitch purl-wise, with yarn in front
- ō **M1P** — Make 1 stitch purl-wise
- **KFB** — Knit into the front and back of the stitch
- ▢ **Pattern Repeat**

- **Right Twist (RT)** — Sl1 to CN, hold in back; K1, K1 from CN
- **Left Twist (LT)** — Sl1 to CN, hold in front; K1, K1 from CN
- **2 over 1 Right Cable (2/1 RC)** — Sl1 to CN, hold in back; K2, K1 from CN
- **2 over 1 Left Cable (2/1 LC)** — Sl2 to CN, hold in front; K1, K2 from CN
- **2 over 1 Right Cable, Purl back (2/1 RPC)** — Sl1 to CN, hold in back; K2, P1 from CN
- **2 over 1 Left Cable, Purl back (2/1 LPC)** — Sl2 to CN, hold in front; P1, K2 from CN
- **2 over 2 Right Cable (2/2 RC)** — Sl2 to CN, hold in back; K2, K2 from CN
- **2 over 2 Left Cable (2/2 LC)** — Sl2 to CN, hold in front; K2, K2 from CN

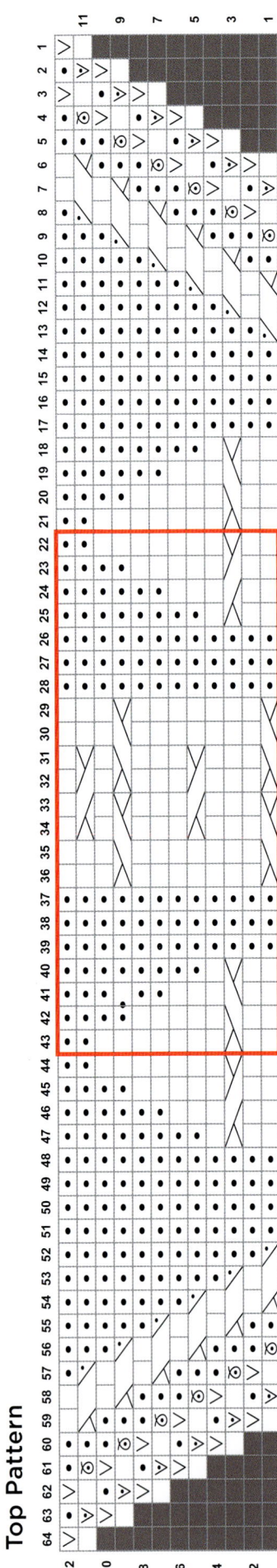

Top Pattern

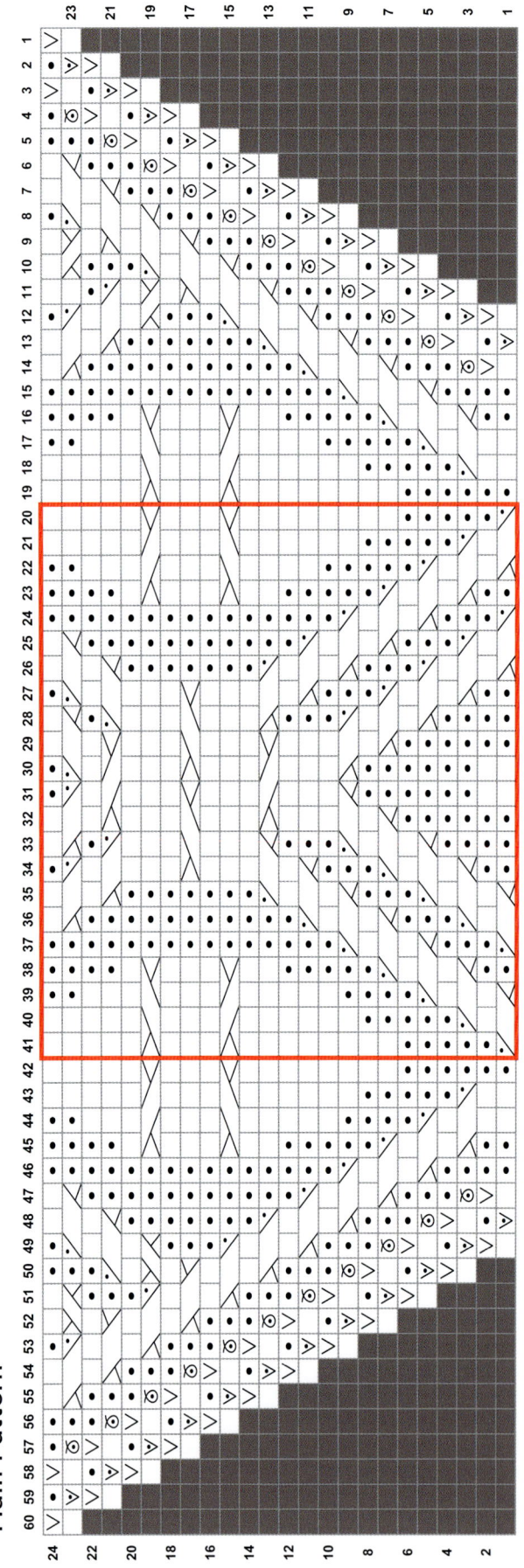

Main Pattern

92　Knots Shawl

BRICKSY JOY SWEATER
by Griselda Zárate

FINISHED MEASUREMENTS
32 (36, 40, 44, 48)(52, 56, 60, 64, 68)" finished chest circumference; meant to be worn with 4" positive ease
Samples are 36/44"; models are 34.5/43"

YARN
City Tweed™ (Aran/heavy worsted weight, 55% Merino Wool, 25% Superfine Alpaca, 20% Donegal Tweed; 164 yards/100g): 7 (8, 9, 9, 10)(11, 12, 13, 14, 14) balls
Size 36" sample Morning Glory 24535
Size 44" sample Harbor Seal 28203

NEEDLES
US 8 (5mm) circular needles (24" or longer), and DPNs or two circular needles for two circulars technique or 32" or longer circular needles for Magic Loop technique, or size to obtain gauge

US 7 (4.5mm) circular needles (24" or longer), and DPNs or two circular needles for two circulars technique or 32" or longer circular needles for Magic Loop technique, or size to obtain gauge

NOTIONS
Yarn Needle
Stitch Markers (13, plus 1 blue and 1 red)
Cable Needle
Stitch Holder or Scrap Yarn

GAUGE
20 sts and 24 rows = 4" in Reverse Stockinette Stitch using larger needles, blocked
20 sts and 24 rnds = 4" in 4x4 Rib in the round using smaller needles, blocked (note that this is approximate due to the amount of stretch in the ribbing)
20 sts and 20 rows = 3.5" in Cable Panel

For pattern support, contact griseldazarate@yahoo.com

Bricksy Joy Sweater

Notes:

With a cropped length and simple silhouette, the Bricksy Joy pullover is a modern interpretation of a cable sweater. It is a classy design that will be a great staple to dress up for a dinner, for an office meeting (even if it is a virtual zoom meeting), or just to wear for a casual get-together.

The Bricksy Joy pullover is worked from the top down, with a 4x4 Rib neckband worked in the round, which is then split into back and front each worked flat, before joining back around for the body. A seamless pattern, it incorporates Reverse Stockinette and a gorgeous textured cable stitch pattern in front and back, as well on the sleeves.

Chart is worked both in the round and flat. When working chart in the round, read each chart row from right to left as a RS row; when working chart flat, read RS rows (odd numbers) from right to left, and WS rows (even numbers) from left to right.

Work sts as presented means to knit the stitches which appear as knit stitches and purl the stitches which appear as purl stitches, on the side that's currently being worked.

4/4 RC (4 over 4 Right Cable)
Sl4 to CN, hold in back; K4, K4 from CN.

4/4 LC (4 over 4 Left Cable)
Sl4 to CN, hold in front; K4, K4 from CN.

DS (Double Stitch)
Made when working German Short Rows; see *Glossary*.

4x4 Rib (in the round over a multiple of 8 sts)
All **Rnds**: (K4, P4) to end.
Note: For an even look, work the last couple of knit sts and the first couple of purl sts of the rib pattern tighter.

Bricksy Joy Cable (flat)
Row 1 (RS): (P to M, SM, 4/4 RC twice, K4, SM) three times, P to end.
Row 2 (WS): (K to M, P to M) three times, K to end.
Row 3: (P to M, K to M) three times, P to end.
Rows 4-9: Rep Rows 2-3.
Row 10: Rep Row 2.
Row 11 (RS): (P to M, SM, K4, 4/4 LC twice, SM) three times, P to end.
Row 12-20: Rep Rows 2-10.
Rep Rows 1-20 for pattern.

Bricksy Joy Cable (in the round)
Rnd 1: (P to M, SM, 4/4 RC twice, K4, SM) to end.
Rnds 2-10: (P to M, K to M) to end.
Rnd 11: (P to M, SM, K4, 4/4 LC twice, SM) to end.
Rnds 12-20: Rep Rnds 2-10.
Rep Rnds 1-20 for pattern.

DIRECTIONS

With smaller needles and using Long Tail Cast On method, CO 88 (88, 104, 104, 104)(104, 104, 104, 104, 104) sts, join in the rnd without twisting sts, PM for BOR.

Neckband
Work 4x4 Rib for 2".

Divide for Body
Remove M and place first 44 (44, 52, 52, 52)(52, 52, 52, 52, 52) sts on a st holder or scrap yarn to work Upper Front later. 44 (44, 52, 52, 52)(52, 52, 52, 52, 52) sts remain on needles for Upper Back.

Upper Back
This section is worked in rows instead of rnds. German Short Rows are used to shape back neck and shoulders.
Using Backward Loop Cast On method, CO 21 (21, 20, 23, 23)(23, 24, 26, 28, 29) sts, turn.
Change to larger needles.
Setup Row (WS): K5 (5, 8, 11, 11)(11, 12, 14, 16, 17), P20, PM, K8, P20, K8, PM, P to end.
Using Backward Loop Cast On method, CO 21 (21, 20, 23, 23)(23, 24, 26, 28, 29) sts. 86 (86, 92, 98, 98)(98, 100, 104, 108, 110) sts.

Back Neck & Shoulders Shaping
Short Row 1 (RS): P5 (5, 8, 11, 11)(11, 12, 14, 16, 17), K20 sts, SM, work sts as presented to M, SM, K3, turn.
Short Row 2 (WS): Make DS, P2, SM, work sts as presented to M, SM, P3, turn.
Short Row 3: Make DS, K to M, SM, work sts as presented to M, SM, K to DS, K DS (always work DS tog as 1st), K3, turn.
Short Row 4: Make DS, P to M, SM, work sts as presented to M, SM, P to DS, P DS, P3, turn.
Short Rows 5-8: Rep Short Rows 3-4 two more times. (Note that Short Row 5 includes cables in central panel.)
Short Row 9: Make DS, K to M, SM, P8, K4, 4/4 LC twice, P8, SM, K to DS, K DS, K3, turn.
Short Row 10: Make DS, P to M, SM, work sts as presented to M, SM, P to DS, P DS, P3, turn.
Short Row 11: Make DS, K to M, SM, work sts as presented to M, SM, K to DS, K DS, K0 (0, 2, 5, 5)(5, 6, 8, 10, 11), P to end.
Short Row 12: K5 (5, 8, 11, 11)(11, 12, 14, 16, 17), P20, SM, work sts as presented to M, SM, P to DS, P DS, P0 (0, 2, 5, 5)(5, 6, 8, 10, 11), K to end. Remove Ms.

Armhole Back
Setup Row 1 (RS): Work all sts as presented.
Setup Row 2 (WS): Work all sts as presented.
Rep Setup Rows 1-2 two more times. PMs at each side of K st panels in last Setup Row 1 rep, slipping Ms on following Setup Row 2.
Work Bricksy Joy Cable (flat) from chart or written instructions, working Rows 1-20 once.
Rep pattern Rows 1 through 18 (14, 16, 20, 20)(20, 20, 20, 20, 20), then rep Rows 1 through - (-, -, 4, 2)(4, 2, 2, 2, 4) once more.

46 (42, 44, 52, 50)(52, 50, 50, 50, 52) rows have been worked; armhole edge measures 7.75 (7, 7.25, 8.5, 8.25)(8.5, 8.25, 8.25, 8.25, 8.5)".

Armhole Back Shaping

Sizes 32 (36, 40, -, -)(-, -, -, -, -)" Only
Row 1 (RS): P1, PFB, work pattern as established to last 2 sts, PFB, P1. 2 sts inc.
Row 2 (WS): Work pattern as established.
Rep Rows 1-2 another 0 (1, 1, -, -,)(-, -, -, -, -) times, continuing Bricksy Joy Cable as established. 88 (90, 96, 98, 98)(98, 100, 104, 108, 110) sts.

Sizes - (36, 40, 44, 48)(52, 56, 60, 64, 68)" Only
Next Row (RS): P1, PFB twice, work pattern as established to last 3 sts, PFB twice, P1. 4 sts inc.
Next Row (WS): Work pattern as established.
Rep last two rows - (1, 2, 2, 4)(5, 7, 5, 5, 5) more times, continuing Bricksy Joy Cable as established. 88 (98, 108, 110, 118)(122, 132, 128, 132, 134) sts.

Sizes - (-, -, -, -)(-, -, 60, 64, 68)" Only
Next Row (RS): P1, (PFB) three times, work pattern as established to last 4 sts, (PFB) three times, P1. 6 sts inc.
Next Row (WS): Work pattern as established.
Rep last two rows - (-, -, -, -)(-, -, 2, 2, 3) more times, continuing Bricksy Joy Cable as established. 88 (98, 108, 110, 118)(122, 132, 146, 150, 158) sts.

Bricksy Joy Cable Row 12 (10, 6, 2, 20)(16, 14, 12, 12, 8) is last row worked. Armhole edge measures 8 (8.25, 9, 9.75, 10)(10.75, 11, 11.25, 11.25, 12)"; 48 (50, 54, 58, 60)(64, 66, 68, 68, 72) rows have been worked.
Place sts on a st holder or scrap yarn to work Body later. Break yarn, leaving a 6-8" long tail.

Upper Front

Setup Row 1 (RS): Remove stitch holder or scrap yarn and place 44 (44, 52, 52, 52)(52, 52, 52, 52, 52) Neckband sts on working needle. With RS facing beginning at Right Shoulder, with larger needles join yarn and PU and P 5 (5, 8, 11, 11)(11, 12, 14, 16, 17) sts, PU and K 16 (16, 12, 12, 12)(12, 12, 12, 12, 12) sts, and K4 (4, 8, 8, 8)(8, 8, 8, 8, 8), PM, P8, K20, P8, PM, K4 (4, 8, 8, 8)(8, 8, 8, 8, 8); PU and K 16 (16, 12, 12, 12)(12, 12, 12, 12, 12) sts, PU and P 5 (5, 8, 11, 11)(11, 12, 14, 16, 17) sts, turn. 86 (86, 92, 98, 98)(98, 100, 104, 108, 110) sts. If desired, PU and K 1 st extra at each side of Neckband sts to avoid a hole, dec this st in following row.

Bricksy Joy Cable—in the round

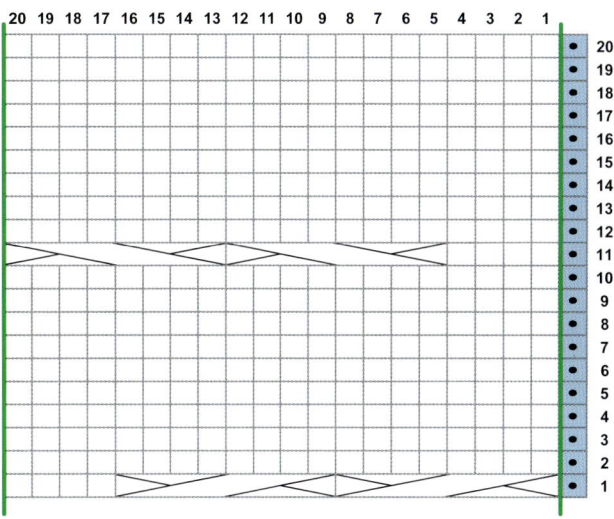

Bricksy Joy Cable—flat

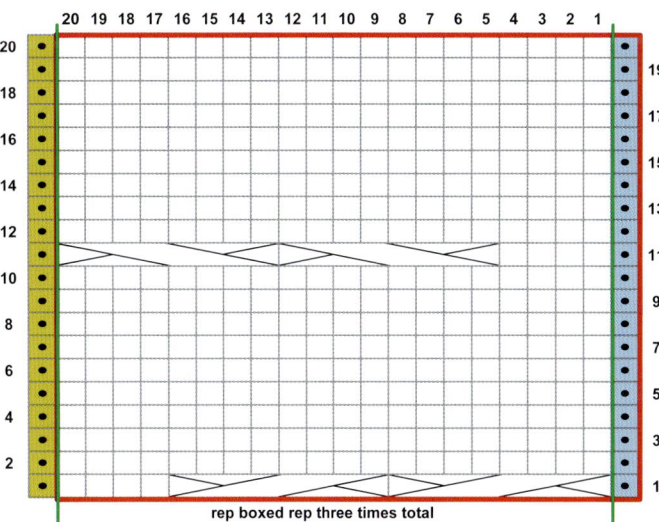

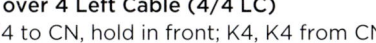
4 over 4 Right Cable (4/4 RC)
Sl4 to CN, hold in back; K4, K4 from CN

4 over 4 Left Cable (4/4 LC)
Sl4 to CN, hold in front; K4, K4 from CN

LEGEND

- ▨ Work All Stitches to Marker
- ▨ Work All Stitches to End
- **K** — RS: Knit stitch / WS: Purl stitch
- **P** — RS: Purl stitch / WS: Knit stitch
- ▢ Pattern Repeat
- | Slip Marker

Left Shoulder Shaping

Short Row 1 (WS): K TBL 5 (5, 8, 11, 11)(11, 12, 14, 16, 17) sts, P to M, SM, K1, turn.
Short Row 2 (RS): Make DS, SM, K3, turn.
Short Row 3: Make DS, P to M, SM, K DS, K1, turn.
Short Row 4: Make DS, P to M, SM, K to DS, K DS, K3, turn.
Short Row 5: Make DS, P to M, SM, K to DS, K DS, K2, turn.
Short Row 6: Make DS, P to M, SM, K to DS, K DS, K3, turn.
Short Row 7: Make DS, P to M, SM, K to DS, K DS, K2, turn.
Short Row 8: Make DS, P to M, SM, K to DS, K DS, K3, turn.
Short Row 9: Make DS, P to M, SM, K to DS, K DS, K1, turn.
Short Row 10: Make DS, P to M, SM, K to DS, K DS, K6, turn.
Short Row 11: Make DS, P to M, SM, K to DS, K DS, K1, turn.
Short Row 12: Make DS, P to M, SM, K to DS, K DS, work sts as presented to end.
Short Row 13: Work sts as presented to M, SM, K to DS, K DS, work sts as presented to end, slipping M, and being careful to dec extra st if increased when picking up sts.

Right Shoulder Shaping

Short Row 1 (RS): P5 (5, 8, 11, 11)(11, 12, 14, 16, 17) sts, K to M, SM, P1, turn.
Short Row 2 (WS): Make DS, SM, P3, turn.
Short Row 3: Make DS, K to M, SM, P DS, P1, turn.
Short Row 4: Make DS, K to M, SM, P to DS, P DS, P3, turn.
Short Row 5: Make DS, K to M, SM, P to DS, P DS, P2, turn.
Short Row 6: Make DS, K to M, SM, P to DS, P DS, P3, turn.
Short Row 7: Make DS, K to M, SM, P to DS, P DS, P2, turn.
Short Row 8: Make DS, K to M, SM, P to DS, P DS, P3, turn.
Short Row 9: Make DS, K to M, SM, P to DS, P DS, P1, turn.
Short Row 10: Make DS, K to M, SM, P to DS, P DS, P6, turn.
Short Row 11: Make DS, K to M, SM, P to DS, P DS, P1, turn.
Short Row 12: Make DS, K to M, SM, P to DS, P DS, work sts as presented to end.
Short Row 13: Work sts as presented to M, remove M, P to DS, P DS, work sts as presented to end, removing M.

Armhole Front

Setup Row 1 (RS): Work all sts as presented.
Setup Row 2 (WS): Work all sts as presented.
Rep Setup Rows 1–2 once, then Setup Row 1 one more time. PMs at each side of K st panels in last Setup Row 2.

Work Bricksy Joy Cable Rows 1–20.
Rep Bricksy Joy Cable Rows 1 through 18 (14, 16, 20, 20)(20, 20, 20, 20, 20), then rep first - (-, -, 4, 2)(4, 2, 2, 2, 4) rows of pattern once more.
46 (42, 44, 52, 50)(52, 50, 50, 50, 52) rows have been worked; armhole edge measures 7.75 (7, 7.25, 8.5, 8.25)(8.5, 8.25, 8.25, 8.25, 8.5)".

Armhole Front Shaping

Sizes 32 (36, 40, -, -)(-, -, -, -, -)" Only
Row 1 (RS): P1, PFB, work pattern as established to last 2 sts, PFB, P1. 2 sts inc.
Row 2 (WS): Work pattern as established.
Rep Rows 1–2 another 0 (1, 1, -, -)(-, -, -, -, -) time, continuing Bricksy Joy Cable as established. 88 (90, 96, 98, 98)(98, 100, 104, 108, 110) sts.

Sizes - (36, 40, 44, 48)(52, 56, 60, 64, 68)" Only
Next Row (RS): P1, (PFB) twice, work pattern as established to last 3 sts, (PFB) twice, P1. 4 sts inc.
Next Row (WS): Work pattern as established.
Rep last two rows - (1, 2, 2, 4)(5, 7, 5, 5, 5) more times, continuing Bricksy Joy Cable as established. 88 (98, 108, 110, 118)(122, 132, 128, 132, 134) sts.

Sizes - (-, -, -, -)(-, -, 60, 64, 68)" Only
Next Row (RS): P1, (PFB) three times, work pattern as established to last 4 sts, (PFB) three times, P1. 6 sts inc.
Next Row (WS): Work pattern as established.
Rep last two rows - (-, -, -, -)(-, -, 2, 2, 3) more times, continuing Bricksy Joy Cable as established. 88 (98, 108, 110, 118)(122, 132, 146, 150, 158) sts.

Bricksy Joy Cable Row 20 (2, 6, 10, 12)(16, 18, 20, 20, 2) is last row worked. Armhole edge measures 8 (8.25, 8.75, 9.5, 9.75)(10.5, 10.75, 11.25, 11.25, 11.75)" and 48 (50, 54, 58, 60)(64, 66, 68, 68, 72) rows have been worked.

Body

Join Back & Front

This section is worked in the rnd.
Rnd 1: Work pattern as established from where last section ended, starting Bricksy Joy Cable (in the round) chart or written instructions on Rnd 1 (3, 7, 11, 13)(17, 19, 1, 1, 3), to end of front sts; using Backward Loop Cast On method, CO 0 (0, 0, 8, 10)(16, 16, 12, 18, 20) sts for left underarm; remove scrap yarn or st holder, join back and work pattern as established (same Rnd number as front) to end; using Backward Loop Cast On method, CO 0 (0, 0, 8, 10)(16, 16, 12, 18, 20) sts for right underarm. PM for BOR. 176 (196, 216, 236, 256)(276, 296, 316, 336, 356) sts.

Work Bricksy Joy Cable, continuing as established then repeating Rnds 1–20, until piece measures 16 (16, 19.25, 19.25, 19.25)(19.25, 22.75, 22.75, 22.75, 22.75)" from shoulder, ending on Rnd 8 for all sizes.

Bottom Edge

Change to smaller needles. Place a locking M at left side (below underarm).

Sizes - (36, -, 44, -)(52, -, 60, -, 68)" Only
Dec Rnd: (P to M, SM, K to M, SM) three times, P to left side M, SM, P1, (P2tog) twice, (P to M, SM, K to M, SM) three times, P to 4 sts before BOR, (P2tog) twice. - (192, -, 232, -)(272, -, 312, -, 352) sts.

Resume All Sizes

Remove all Ms (except for BOR) during first rnd.
Work 4x4 Rib for 2".
Total garment length is 18 (18, 21.25, 21.25, 21.25)(21.25, 24.75, 24.75, 24.75, 24.75)".
BO in pattern.

Sleeves (make two the same)

Sleeves are worked in the rnd. With RS facing, using larger needles, beginning from mid-underarm and skipping 1 st as necessary, PU and K 32 (33, 37, 39, 42)(44, 45, 48, 48, 50) sts, PM (blue color), PU and K 20 sts, PM (red color), PU and K 32 (33, 37, 39, 42)(44, 45, 48, 48, 50) sts. 84 (86, 94, 98, 104)(108, 110, 116, 116, 120) sts.

Sleeve Cap Shaping

Short Row 1 (RS): P to blue M, SM, K to red M, SM, P3, turn.
Short Row 2 (WS): Make DS, K to red M, SM, P to blue M, SM, K3, turn.
Short Row 3: Make DS, P to blue M, SM, K to red M, SM, P to DS, P DS, P3, turn.
Short Row 4: Make DS, K to red M, SM, P to blue M, SM, K to DS, K DS, K3, turn.
Rep Short Rows 3–4 three more times. Resume working in the rnd.
Next Rnd: Work sts as presented, including last DS.

Sleeve Shaping

Work Bricksy Joy Cable Rnds 1–20 and at the same time work Dec Rnds.
Dec Rnd: P2, P2tog, P to blue M, SM, work as established to M, SM, P to last 4 sts, P2tog, P2. 2 sts dec.
Rep Dec Rnd every 6 (6, 5, 5, 4)(4, 4, 4, 4, 4) rnds, 17 (17, 19, 20, 22)(23, 23, 24, 24, 25) more times. 48 (50, 54, 56, 58)(60, 62, 66, 66, 68) sts.
WE in pattern as established until piece measures 20" from shoulder, or desired sleeve length.

Cuff

Change to smaller needles.

Sizes - (36, -, -, 48)(-, -, 60, 64, -)" Only
Dec Rnd: P2tog, P to M, SM, K to M, SM, P to last 2 sts, P2tog. - (48, -, -, 56)(-, -, 64, 64, -) sts.

Size - (-, 40, -, -)(-, -, -, -, -)" Only
Dec Rnd: (P2tog) three times, P to M, SM, K to M, SM, P to last 6 sts, (P2tog) three times. 48 sts.

Sizes - (-, -, -, -)(52, -, -, -, 68)" Only
Dec Rnd: (P2tog) twice, P to M, SM, K to M, SM, P to last 4 sts, (P2tog) twice. - (-, -, -, -)(56, -, -, -, 64) sts.

Size - (-, -, -, -)(-, 56, -, -, -)" Only
Inc Rnd: PFB, P to M, SM, K to M, SM, P to last st, PFB. 64 sts.

Resume All Sizes

48 (48, 48, 56, 56)(56, 64, 64, 64, 64) sts.
Work 4x4 Rib for 2 (2, 2, 2.5, 2.5)(2.5, 2.5, 2.5, 2.5, 2.5)".
BO in pattern.

Finishing

Weave in ends, wash, and block to measurements or to achieve desired results.

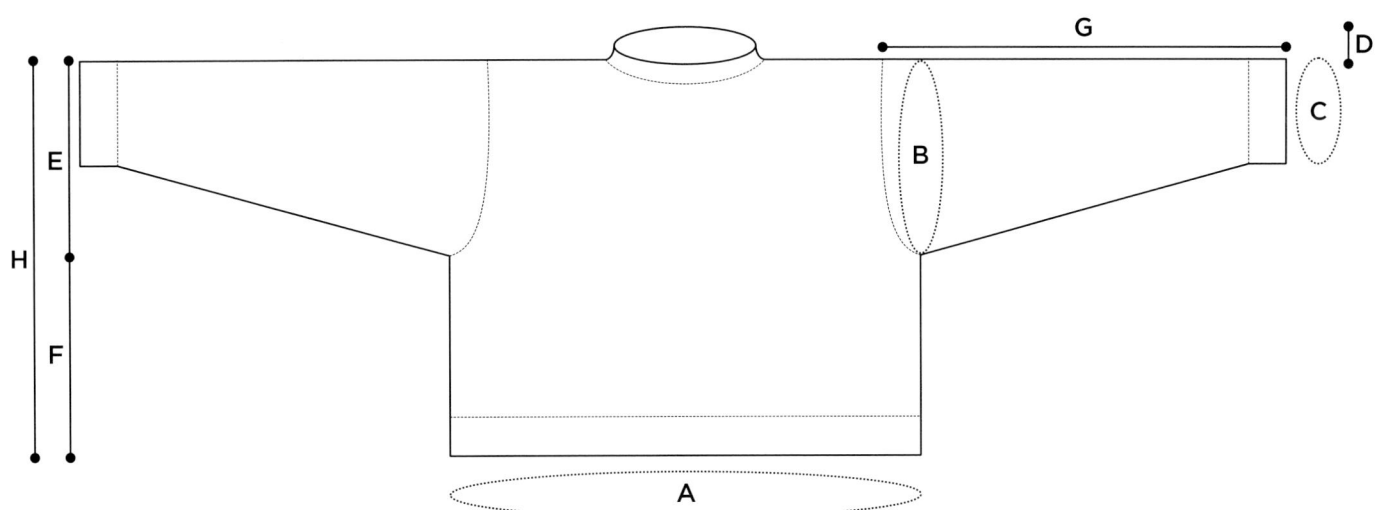

- **A** *chest circumference* 32 (36, 40, 44, 48)(52, 56, 60, 64, 68)"
- **B** *upper arm circumference* 16 (16.5, 18, 19, 20)(21, 21.5, 22.5, 22.5, 23.5)"
- **C** *wrist circumference* 9.5 (9.5, 9.5, 11.25, 11.25)(11.25, 12.75, 12.75, 12.75, 12.75)"
- **D** *front neck drop* 2"
- **E** *armhole length* 8 (8.25, 9, 9.5, 10)(10.5, 10.75, 11.25, 11.25, 11.75)"
- **F** *body length to underarm* 10 (9.75, 12.25, 11.75, 11.25)(10.75, 14, 13.5, 13.5, 13)"
- **G** *sleeve length* 22 (22, 22, 22.5, 22.5)(22.5, 22.5, 22.5, 22.5, 22.5)"
- **H** *total body length* 18 (18, 21.25, 21.25, 21.25)(21.25, 24.75, 24.75, 24.75, 24.75)"

PINBALL VEST
by Sandi Rosner

FINISHED MEASUREMENTS
34.25 (37.5, 41.75, 45, 48)(52.25, 55.5, 58.5, 62.75, 66)" finished chest circumference; meant to be worn with 4–6" positive ease
Samples are 37.5/45"; models are 34.5/43"

YARN
Capra™ (DK weight, 85% Merino Wool, 15% Cashmere; 123 yards/50g): 8 (9, 10, 11, 12)(13, 14, 15, 17, 18) balls
Size 37.5" sample White 27656
Size 45" sample Tansy Heather 27661

NEEDLES
US 6 (4mm) 16" and 24–32" circular needles, or size to obtain gauge

NOTIONS
Yarn Needle
Stitch Markers
Scrap Yarn or Stitch Holders
Cable Needle

GAUGE
21 sts and 32 rnds = 4" in Reverse Stockinette Stitch in the round, blocked
30 sts and 32 rnds = 4" in Lattice Cable in the round, blocked

For pattern support, contact rosnersandi@gmail.com

Pinball Vest

Notes:
The lines of the cable pattern on the Pinball Vest bounce back and forth between vertical ribs like the little silver balls bouncing between the paddles on a classic pinball game.

The body of the Pinball Vest is knit in the round from the lower edge to the armholes, then divided and worked flat to the neck. Increases in the upper body push the shoulder line outward. Shoulders are shaped with German Short Rows for a relaxed, flattering fit.

Chart is worked both in the round and flat. When working chart in the round, read each chart row from right to left as a RS row; when working chart flat, read RS rows (odd numbers) from right to left, and WS rows (even numbers) from left to right.

2/2 LC (2 over 2 Left Cable)
Sl2 to CN, hold in front; K2, K2 from CN.

2/2 RC (2 over 2 Right Cable)
Sl2 to CN, hold in back; K2, K2 from CN.

2/2 LPC (2 over 2 Left Cable, Purl back)
Sl2 to CN, hold in front; P2, K2 from CN.

2/2 RPC (2 over 2 Right Cable, Purl back)
Sl2 to CN, hold in back; K2, P2 from CN.

M1P (Make 1 Purl)
Inserting LH needle from back to front, PU the horizontal strand between the st just worked and the next st, and P TFL.

DS (Double Stitch)
Made when working German Short Rows; see *Glossary*.

Lattice Cable (in the round over a multiple of 28 sts plus 2)
Setup Rnd: *(K2, P2) three times, K6, (P2, K2) two times, P2; rep from * to last 2 sts, K2.
Rnd 1: (K2, P4, 2/2 RPC twice, K2, 2/2 LPC twice, P4) to last 2 sts, K2.
Rnd 2: *K2, P4, (K2, P2) four times, K2, P4; rep from * to last 2 sts, K2.
Rnd 3: (K2, P2, 2/2 RPC twice, P2, K2, P2, 2/2 LPC twice, K2) to last 2 sts, K2.
Rnd 4: *(K2, P2) two times, (K2, P4) two times, (K2, P2) two times; rep from * to last 2 sts, K2.
Rnd 5: (K2, 2/2 RPC twice, P4, K2, P4, 2/2 LPC twice) to last 2 sts, K2.
Rnd 6: *K4, P2, K2, (P6, K2) two times, P2, K2; rep from * to last 2 sts, K2.
Rnd 7: (K4, 2/2 RPC, P6, K2, P6, 2/2 LPC, K2) to last 2 sts, K2.
Rnd 8: (K6, P8, K2, P8, K4) to last 2 sts, K2.
Rnd 9: (K2, 2/2 LC, P8, K2, P8, 2/2 RC) to last 2 sts, K2.
Rnd 10: Rep Rnd 8.
Rnd 11: (K4, 2/2 LPC, P6, K2, P6, 2/2 RPC, K2) to last 2 sts, K2.
Rnd 12: Rep Rnd 6.
Rnd 13: (K2, 2/2 LPC twice, P4, K2, P4, 2/2 RPC twice) to last 2 sts, K2.
Rnd 14: Rep Rnd 4.
Rnd 15: (K2, P2, 2/2 LPC twice, P2, K2, P2, 2/2 RPC twice, P2) to last 2 sts, K2.
Rnd 16: Rep Rnd 2.
Rnd 17: (K2, P4, 2/2 LPC twice, K2, 2/2 RPC twice, P4) to last 2 sts, K2.
Rnd 18: (K2, P6, K2, P2, K6, P2, K2, P6) to last 2 sts, K2.
Rnd 19: (K2, P6, 2/2 LPC, K6, 2/2 RPC, P6) to last 2 sts, K2.
Rnd 20: (K2, P8, K10, P8) to last 2 sts, K2.
Rnd 21: (K2, P8, 2/2 RC, K2, 2/2 LC, P8) to last 2 sts, K2.
Rnd 22: Rep Rnd 20.
Rnd 23: (K2, P6, 2/2 RPC, K6, 2/2 LPC, P6) to last 2 sts, K2.
Rnd 24: Rep Rnd 18
Rep Rnds 1–24 for pattern.

Lattice Cable (flat over a multiple of 28 sts plus 2)
Row 1 (RS): (K2, P4, 2/2 RPC twice, K2, 2/2 LPC twice, P4) to last 2 sts, K2.
Row 2 (WS): P2, *K4, (P2, K2) four times, P2, K4, P2; rep from * to end.
Row 3: (K2, P2, 2/2 RPC twice, P2, K2, P2, 2/2 LPC twice, K2) to last 2 sts, K2.
Row 4: P2, *(K2, P2) two times, (K4, P2) two times, (K2, P2) two times; rep from * to end.
Row 5: (K2, 2/2 RPC twice, P4, K2, P4, 2/2 LPC twice) to last 2 sts, K2.
Row 6: P2, *P2, K2, (P2, K6) two times, P2, K2, P4; rep from * to end.
Row 7: (K4, 2/2 RPC, P6, K2, P6, 2/2 LPC, K2) to last 2 sts, K2.
Row 8: P2, (P4, K8, P2, K8, P6) to end.
Row 9: (K2, 2/2 LC, P8, K2, P8, 2/2 RC) to last 2 sts, K2.
Row 10: Rep Row 8.
Row 11: (K4, 2/2 LPC, P6, K2, P6, 2/2 RPC, K2) to last 2 sts, K2.
Row 12: Rep Row 6.
Row 13: (K2, 2/2 LPC twice, P4, K2, P4, 2/2 RPC twice) to last 2 sts, K2.
Row 14: Rep Row 4.
Row 15: (K2, P2, 2/2 LPC twice, P2, K2, P2, 2/2 RPC twice, P2) to last 2 sts, K2.
Row 16: Rep Row 2.
Row 17: (K2, P4, 2/2 LPC twice, K2, 2/2 RPC twice, P4) to last 2 sts, K2.
Row 18: P2, (K6, P2, K2, P6, K2, P2, K6, P2) to end.
Row 19: (K2, P6, 2/2 LPC, K6, 2/2 RPC, P6) to last 2 sts, K2.
Row 20: P2, (K8, P10, K8, P2) to end.
Row 21: (K2, P8, 2/2 RC, K2, 2/2 LC, P8) to last 2 sts, K2.
Row 22: Rep Row 20.
Row 23: (K2, P6, 2/2 RPC, K6, 2/2 LPC, P6) to last 2 sts, K2.
Row 24: Rep Row 18.
Rep Rows 1–24 for pattern.

DIRECTIONS

Hem
Using longer circular needles, CO 232 (248, 288, 304, 320)(360, 376, 392, 432, 448) sts. Join to work in the rnd, being careful not to twist sts; PM for BOR.
Rnd 1: *K1, P2, (K2, P2) 3 (4, 3, 4, 5)(4, 5, 6, 5, 6) times, PM, **(K2, P2) three times, K6, (P2, K2) two times, P2; rep from ** 2 (2, 3, 3, 3)(4, 4, 4, 5, 5) more times, K2, PM, (P2, K2) 3 (4, 3, 4, 5)(4, 5, 6, 5, 6) times, P2, K1, PM; rep from * once more.
Work knits and purls as established in Rnd 1 until piece measures 1.5″.

Body
Rnd 1: (P to M, SM, work Lattice Cable to M, SM, P to M) two times.
Rep Rnd 1 until piece measures 13.5″ from CO edge, ending with an even-numbered rnd of pattern.

Armholes & V-Neck Division
Next Rnd: P to M, SM, work 42 (42, 56, 56, 56)(70, 70, 70, 84, 84) sts in pattern as established, KFB, place 59 (63, 73, 77, 81)(91, 95, 99, 109, 113) sts just worked on scrap yarn or st holder for Left Front, KFB, work in pattern to M, SM, P to M, place 59 (63, 73, 77, 81)(91, 95, 99, 109, 113) sts just worked on scrap yarn or st holder for Right Front, work in pattern to end. 116 (124, 144, 152)(160, 180, 188, 196, 216, 224) sts remain for Back. Make note of last row of Lattice Cable worked.

Back
Next Row (WS): K to M, SM, work Lattice Cable as established to M, SM, K to end. 116 (124, 144, 152)(160, 180, 188, 196, 216, 224) sts.
Work four more rows in Rev St st and Lattice Cable as established.

Armhole Shaping
Inc Row (RS): P to 1 st before M, M1P, P1, SM, work Lattice Cable to M, SM, P1, M1P, P to end. 2 sts inc.
Rep Inc Row every eight rows five more times. 128 (136, 156, 164, 172)(192, 200, 208, 228, 236) sts.
WE until armholes measure 7 (7, 7.5, 7.5, 8)(8, 8.5, 8.5, 9, 9)″ from division, ending with a WS row.

Shoulder Shaping
Note: Maintain Lattice Cable as much as possible while shaping shoulders. If there are not enough sts to complete a cable, work the extra sts in St st.
Short Row 1 (RS): Work in pattern to last 4 (5, 6, 5, 5)(6, 5, 5, 6, 6) sts, turn.
Short Row 2 (WS): Make DS, work in pattern to last 4 (5, 6, 5, 5)(6, 5, 5, 6, 6) sts, turn.
Short Row 3: Make DS, work in pattern to 3 (4, 5, 4, 4)(5, 4, 4, 5, 5) sts before last DS, turn.
Short Row 4: Make DS, work in pattern to 3 (4, 5, 4, 4)(5, 4, 4, 5, 5) sts before last DS, turn.
Rep Short Rows 3–4 another 2 (2, 2, 6, 4)(4, 4, 0, 4, 0) times.
Next Short Row (RS): Make DS, work in pattern to 4 (4, 5, 5, 5)(6, 5, 5, 6, 6) sts before last DS, turn.
Next Short Row (WS): Make DS, work in pattern to 4 (4, 5, 5, 5)(6, 5, 5, 6, 6) sts before last DS, turn.
Rep last two short rows 3 (3, 3, 1, 3)(3, 5, 9, 5, 9) more times.
Next Row (RS): Work in pattern to end, working all DSs as single sts.
Next Row (WS): Work in pattern to end, working all DSs as single sts.
BO 36 (40, 48, 52, 54)(64, 66, 70, 78, 82) sts, work next 56 (56, 60, 60, 64)(64, 68, 68, 72, 72) sts in pattern and place on scrap yarn or st holder for Back Neck, BO remaining 36 (40, 48, 52, 54)(64, 66, 70, 78, 82) sts.

Left Front
Return left front sts to needle and join yarn at center front for a WS row.
Setup Row (WS): P2, work Lattice Cable as established to M, SM, K to end. 59 (63, 73, 77, 81)(91, 95, 99, 109, 113) sts.

V-Neck Shaping
Note: Armhole shaping begins before V-Neck shaping is complete. Please read ahead.
Maintain Lattice Cable as much as possible while shaping V-Neck. If there are not enough sts to complete a cable, work the extra sts in St st.
Dec Row (RS): Work in pattern to last 3 sts, K2tog, K1. 1 st dec.
Cont in Rev St st and Lattice Cable as established, rep Dec Row every RS row 28 (28, 30, 30, 32)(32, 34, 34, 36, 36) more times.
AT THE SAME TIME, beginning with third Dec Row, shape armhole as follows.

Armhole Shaping
Inc Row (RS): P to 1 st before M, M1P, P1, SM, work Lattice Cable to end, including V-Neck shaping. 1 st inc.
Rep Inc Row every eight rows five more times.
When Armhole and V-Neck shaping are complete, 36 (40, 48, 52, 54)(64, 66, 70, 78, 82) sts remain.

When armhole measures 7 (7, 7.5, 7.5, 8)(8, 8.5, 8.5, 9, 9)″ from division, ending with a RS row, begin shaping shoulder as follows. *Note:* Front neck shaping may not be complete at this point.

Shoulder Shaping
Short Row 1 (WS): Work in pattern to last 4 (5, 6, 5, 5)(6, 5, 5, 6, 6) sts, turn.
Short Row 2 (RS): Make DS, work in pattern to end.
Short Row 3: Work in pattern to 3 (4, 5, 4, 4)(5, 4, 4, 5, 5) sts before last DS, turn.
Short Row 4: Make DS, work in pattern to end.
Rep Short Rows 3–4 another 2 (2, 2, 6, 4)(4, 4, 0, 4, 0) times.
Next Short Row (WS): Work in pattern to 4 (4, 5, 5, 5)(6, 5, 5, 6, 6) sts before last DS, turn.
Next Short Row (RS): Make DS, work in pattern to end.
Rep last two short rows 2 (2, 2, 0, 2)(2, 4, 8, 4, 8) more times.
Next Row (WS): Work in pattern to end, working all DSs as single sts.
BO all sts.

Pinball Vest

Right Front

Return right front sts to needle and join yarn at armhole edge for a WS row.
Setup Row (WS): K to M, SM, work Lattice Cable to last 2 sts, P2. 59 (63, 73, 77, 81)(91, 95, 99, 109, 113) sts.

V-Neck Shaping

Note: Armhole shaping begins before V-Neck shaping is complete. Please read ahead.
Maintain Lattice Cable as much as possible while shaping V-Neck. If there are not enough sts to complete a cable, work the extra sts in St st.
Dec Row (RS): K1, SSK, work in pattern to end. 1 st dec.
Cont in Rev St st and Lattice Cable as established, rep Dec Row every RS row 28 (28, 30, 30, 32)(32, 34, 34, 36, 36) more times.
AT THE SAME TIME, beginning with third Dec Row, shape Armhole as follows.

Armhole Shaping

Inc Row (RS): Work in pattern to M including V-Neck shaping, SM, P1, M1P, P to end. 1 st inc.
Rep Inc Row every eight rows five more times.

When Armhole and V-Neck shaping are complete, 36 (40, 48, 52, 54)(64, 66, 70, 78, 82) sts remain.

When armhole measures 7 (7, 7.5, 7.5, 8)(8, 8.5, 8.5, 9, 9)" from division, ending with a WS row, begin shaping shoulder as follows. *Note:* Front neck shaping may not be complete at this point.

Shoulder Shaping

Short Row 1 (RS): Work in pattern to last 4 (5, 6, 5, 5)(6, 5, 5, 6, 6) sts, turn.
Short Row 2 (WS): Make DS, work in pattern to end.
Short Row 3: Work in pattern to 3 (4, 5, 4, 4)(5, 4, 4, 5, 5) sts before last DS, turn.
Short Row 4: Make DS, work in pattern to end.
Rep Short Rows 3–4 another 2 (2, 2, 6, 4)(4, 4, 0, 4, 0) times.

Next Short Row (RS): Work in pattern to 4 (4, 5, 5, 5)(6, 5, 5, 6, 6) sts before last DS, turn.
Next Short Row (WS): Make DS, work in pattern to end.
Rep last two short rows 2 (2, 2, 0, 2)(2, 4, 8, 4, 8) more times.
Next Row (RS): Work in pattern to end, working all DSs as single sts.
BO all sts.

Finishing

Sew shoulder seams tog using Mattress Stitch or preferred method.

Armhole Edging

Using shorter circular needles, beginning at base of armhole, PU and K 72 (72, 76, 76, 84)(84, 88, 88, 92, 92) sts evenly around armhole. PM for BOR.
Work 2x2 Rib for 1.5".
BO in rib as established.

Neck Edging

Using longer circular needles, beginning at left shoulder seam, PU and K 72 (72, 76, 80, 84)(84, 92, 92, 96, 96) sts down left front neck edge to center of V-neck, PM, PU and K 72 (72, 76, 80, 84)(84, 92, 92, 96, 96) sts up right front neck edge to shoulder seam, slip back neck sts from holder to LH needle and K1, (P2, K2) 13 (13, 14, 14, 15)(15, 16, 16, 17, 17) times, P2, K1. PM for BOR. 200 (200, 212, 220, 232)(232, 252, 252, 264, 264) sts.
Rnd 1: K1, (P2, K2) to 3 sts before M, P1, K2tog, SM, SSK, P1, (K2, P2) to last st, K1. 198 (198, 210, 218, 230)(230, 250, 250, 262, 262) sts.
Rnd 2: Work 2x2 Rib as established.
Rnd 3: Work as established to 2 sts before M, K2tog, SM, SSK, work as established to end. 2 sts dec.
Rnd 4: WE as established.
Rep Rnds 3–4 four more times. 188 (188, 200, 208, 220)(220, 240, 240, 252, 252) sts.
BO in rib.

Weave in ends, wash, and block to measurements or to achieve desired results.

Lattice Cable

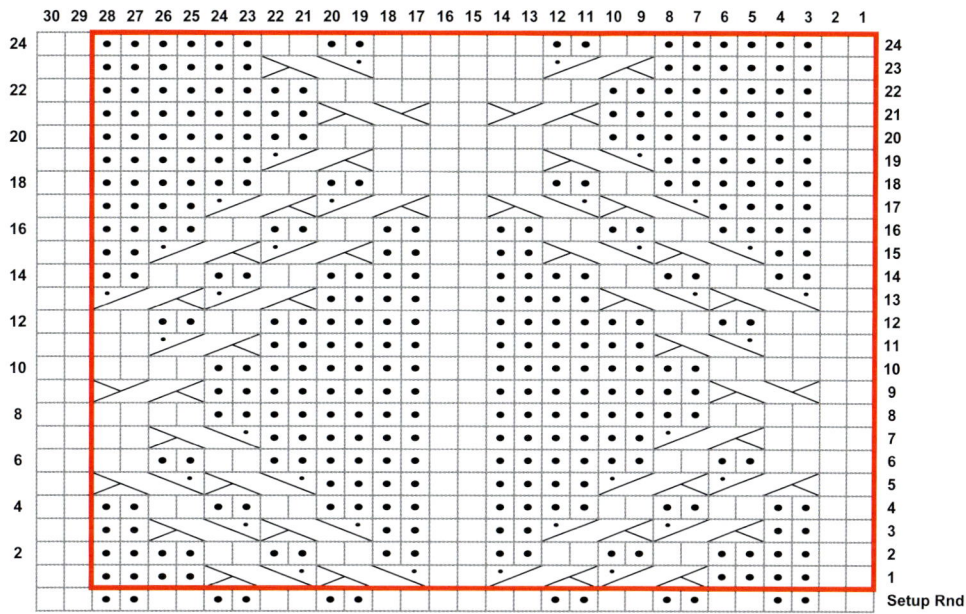

LEGEND

K
RS: Knit stitch
WS: Purl stitch

P
RS: Purl stitch
WS: Knit stitch

2 over 2 Right Cable (2/2 RC)
Sl2 to CN, hold in back; K2, K2 from CN

2 over 2 Left Cable (2/2 LC)
Sl2 to CN, hold in front; K2, K2 from CN

2 over 2 Right Cable, Purl back (2/2 RPC)
Sl2 to CN, hold in back; K2, P2 from CN

2 over 2 Left Cable, Purl back (2/2 LPC)
Sl2 to CN, hold in front; P2, K2 from CN

Pattern Repeat

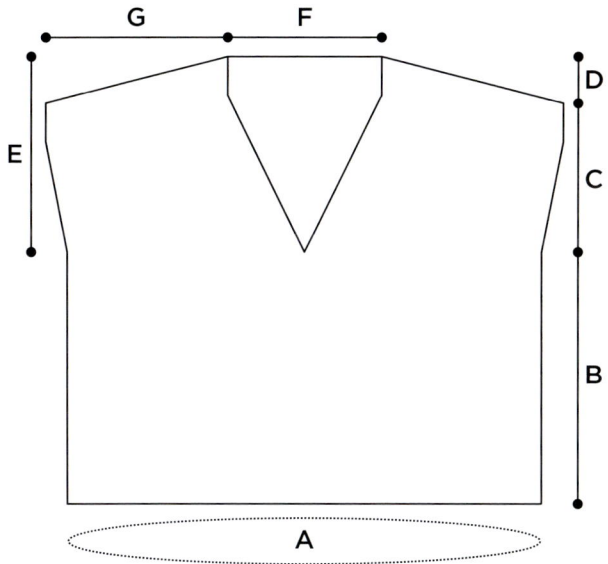

- **A** *body circumference* 34.25 (37.5, 41.75, 44.75, 48) (52.25, 55.5, 58.5, 62.75, 66)"
- **B** *length to armholes* 13.5"
- **C** *armhole depth* 7 (7, 7.5, 7.5, 8)(8, 8.5, 8.5, 9, 9)"
- **D** *shoulder slope* 2 (2, 2, 2.5, 2.5)(2.5, 3, 3, 3, 3)"
- **E** *front neck drop* 9 (9, 9.5, 10, 10.5)(10.5, 11.5, 11.5, 12, 12)"
- **F** *back neck width* 7.5 (7.5, 8, 8, 8.5)(8.5, 9, 9, 9.5, 9.5)"
- **G** *shoulder width* 6 (6.75, 7.5, 8.25, 8.75)(10, 10.5, 11.25, 12, 12.75)"

Pinball Vest

VARJA SWEATER
by Claire Slade

FINISHED MEASUREMENTS
33 (37.25, 41, 45.25, 49)(53.25, 57.75, 61.25, 65.75)" finished chest circumference; meant to be worn with 2-6" positive ease
Sample is 37.25"; model is 34.5"

YARN
Wool of the Andes™ (worsted weight, 100% Peruvian Highland Wool; 110 yards/50g) Amethyst Heather 23900, 9 (9, 10, 12, 12)(14, 15, 16, 17) skeins

NEEDLES
US 7 (4.5mm) 16", 24", and 32" circular needles and DPNs, or size to obtain gauge

US 5 (3.75mm) 16" circular needles and DPNs, or two sizes smaller than size used to obtain gauge

NOTIONS
Yarn Needle
Stitch Markers
Cable Needle
Stitch Holders or Scrap Yarn

GAUGE
18 sts and 22 rnds = 4" in Stockinette Stitch and Cable Pattern, in the round on larger needles, blocked

For pattern support, contact verilyknits@gmail.com

Varja Sweater

Notes:
Varja is a Nordic-inspired sweater with looping cables like forged ironwork that twist around the yoke.

Varja is knit in the round from the top down in one piece. The cabled yoke is worked first then stitches are placed on hold for the sleeves whilst the body is knit. Sleeves are also worked in the round with stitches picked up at the underarm so that the only finishing required is weaving in ends and blocking.

Chart is worked in the round; read each chart row from right to left as a RS row.

Wide Neck vs. Extra Wide Neck
For a standard wide neck (as shown in schematic), use the smaller needle size for the neck, and a Cable Cast On or other method of choice that is not too loose. For an extra wide neck as shown in the sample, use the same needle size as the body; use an extra loose and stretchy cast on method, and then stretch the neck out when blocking.

2/2 LC (2 over 2 Left Cable)
Sl2 to CN, hold in front; K2, K2 from CN.

2/2 RC (2 over 2 Right Cable)
Sl2 to CN, hold in back; K2, K2 from CN.

2/2 LPC (2 over 2 Left Cable, Purl back)
Sl2 to CN, hold in front; P2, K2 from CN.

2/2 RPC (2 over 2 Right Cable, Purl back)
Sl2 to CN, hold in back; K2, P2 from CN.

Varja Cable (in the rnd beginning with a multiple of 12 sts)
Rnd 1: (2/2 RC, K3, M1R, K2, M1L, K3) to end. 2 sts inc per rep.
Rnd 2: K all.
Rnd 3: Sl2, (2/2 LPC, K6, 2/2 RPC) to last 12 sts, 2/2 LPC, K6, 2/2 RPC using last 2 sts of rnd with first 2 slipped sts, keeping BOR M in middle of cable.
Rnd 4: (P4, K4, M1R, K2, M1L, K4) to end. 2 sts inc per rep.
Rnd 5: (P4, 2/2 LPC, K4, 2/2 RPC) to end.
Rnd 6: (P6, K8, P2) to end.
Rnd 7: (P6, 2/2 LPC, 2/2 RPC, P2) to end.
Rnd 8: (P8, K4, P4) to end.
Rnd 9: (P8, 2/2 LC, P4) to end.
Rnd 10: (P8, K4, P4) to end.
Rnd 11: (P6, 2/2 RPC, 2/2 LPC, P2) to end.
Rnd 12: (P6, K2, P4, K2, P2) to end.
Rnd 13: (P4, 2/2 RPC, P4, 2/2 LPC) to end.
Rnd 14: (P4, K2, P8, K2) to end.
Rnd 15: Sl2, (2/2 RPC, P8, 2/2 LPC) to last 14 sts, 2/2 RPC, P8, 2/2 LPC using last 2 sts of rnd with first 2 slipped sts, keeping BOR M in middle of cable.
Rnd 16: (K4, P12) to end.
Rnd 17: (2/2 RC, P12) to end.
Rnd 18: (K4, P12) to end.
Rnd 19: Sl2, (2/2 LC, P8, 2/2 RC) to last 14 sts, 2/2 LC, P8, 2/2 RC using last 2 sts of rnd with first 2 slipped sts, keeping BOR M in middle of cable.
Rnd 20: (K6, P8, K2) to end.
Rnd 21: (K4, 2/2 LC, P4, 2/2 RC) to end.
Rnd 22: (K8, P4, K4) to end.
Rnd 23: (K6, 2/2 LC, 2/2 RC, K2) to end.
Rnd 24: K all.
Rnd 25: (K8, 2/2 LC, K4) to end.
Rnd 26: K all.
Rnd 27: (K6, 2/2 RPC, 2/2 LPC, K2) to end.
Rnds 28–30: (K8, P4, K4) to end.
Rnd 31: (K6, 2/2 LC, 2/2 RC, K2) to end.
Rnd 32: K all.
Rnd 33: (K8, 2/2 LC, K4) to end.

DIRECTIONS

Neck Edge
Using smaller needles for a wide neck or larger needles for an extra wide neck (see *Notes*), CO 104 (116, 120, 120, 120) (128, 124, 128, 128) sts and join to work in the rnd, being careful not to twist sts; PM for BOR.
Work 2x2 Rib for 1".
Change to larger needles.

Yoke Setup
Sizes 33 (-, -, -, -)(-, 57.75, -, -)" Only
Setup Rnd: M1R, K to end. 105 (-, -, -, -)(-, 125, -, -) sts.

Size - (37.25, -, -, -)(-, -, -, -)" Only
Setup Rnd: (M1R, K38) two times, M1R, K to end. 119 sts.

Sizes - (-, 41, -, 49)(-, -, -, -)" Only
Setup Rnd: (M1R, K20) to end. - (-, 126, -, 126)(-, -, -, -) sts.

Size - (-, -, -, -)(53.25, -, -, -)" Only
Setup Rnd: (M1R, K12) ten times, K to end. 138 sts.

Size - (-, -, -, -)(-, -, 61.25, -)" Only
Setup Rnd: (M1R, K18) seven times, K to end. 135 sts.

Size - (-, -, -, -)(-, -, -, 65.75)" Only
Setup Rnd: (M1R, K7) 17 times, K to end. 145 sts.

Resume All Sizes
Knit 1 (1, 1, 2, 2)(2, 2, 2, 2) rnds.

Yoke
Sizes 33 (37.25, 41, -, -)(-, -, -, -)" Only
Inc Rnd: (K7, M1L) to end. 120 (136, 144, -, -)(-, -, -, -) sts.
Knit one rnd.

Sizes - (-, -, -, -)(-, 57.75, 61.25, 65.75)" Only
Inc Rnd: (K3, M1R, K2) to end. - (-, -, -, -)(-, 150, 162, 174) sts.
Knit - (-, -, -, -)(-, 2, 2, 3) rnds.

Sizes - (-, -, 45.25, 49)(53.25, 57.75, 61.25, 65.75)" Only
Inc Rnd: (K4, M1R, K2, M1L) to end. - (-, -, 160, 168)(184, 200, 216, 232) sts.
Knit - (-, -, 2, 2)(3, 3, 3, 3) rnds.

Resume All Sizes
Next Inc Rnd: (K5, M1R, K2, M1L, K1) to end. 150 (170, 180, 200, 210)(230, 250, 270, 290) sts.
Knit 1 (1, 1, 2, 2)(3, 3, 4, 4) rnds.

Next Inc Rnd: (K6, M1R, K2, M1L, K2) to end. 180 (204, 216, 240, 252)(276, 300, 324, 348) sts.
Knit 1 (1, 2, 2, 3)(3, 3, 4, 5) rnds.

Work Rnds 1–33 of Varja Cable from chart or written instructions. 240 (272, 288, 320, 336)(368, 400, 432, 464) sts.
Knit 2 (2, 2, 3, 3)(4, 4, 5, 5) rnds.

Sleeves Separation
Next Rnd: *K70 (80, 86, 96, 102)(112, 122, 130, 140), place next 50 (56, 58, 64, 66)(72, 78, 86, 92) sts on st holder or scrap yarn for sleeve, CO 4 (4, 6, 6, 8)(8, 8, 8, 8) sts; rep from * once more. 148 (168, 184, 204, 220)(240, 260, 276, 296) sts.

Body
Work St st until piece measures 16 (16, 17, 18, 18)(19, 19, 20, 20)" from underarm, or desired length.

Lower Edge
Change to smaller needles.
Work 2x2 Rib for 1".
BO all sts in pattern.

Sleeves (make two the same)
With RS facing, return held 50 (56, 58, 64, 66)(72, 78, 86, 92) sts to larger needle and rejoin yarn.
PU and K 2 (2, 3, 3, 4)(4, 4, 4, 4) sts, PM for BOR, PU and K 2 (2, 3, 3, 4)(4, 4, 4, 4) sts, K to end. 54 (60, 64, 70, 74)(80, 86, 94, 100) sts.

Knit 14 (10, 10, 7, 7)(5, 4, 4, 3) rnds.
Dec Rnd: K1, K2tog, K to last 3 sts, SSK, K1. 2 sts dec.
Rep these 15 (11, 11, 8, 8)(6, 5, 5, 4) rnds 4 (7, 7, 10, 10)(13, 14, 16, 19) more times. 44 (44, 48, 48, 52)(52, 56, 60, 60) sts.
Work St st until sleeve measures 18.5 (19, 19, 19.5, 19.5)(20, 20, 20, 20)" or desired length.

Change to smaller needles.
Work 2x2 Rib for 1".
BO all sts in pattern.

Finishing
Weave in all ends, wash, and block to measurements or to achieve desired results.

Varja Cable

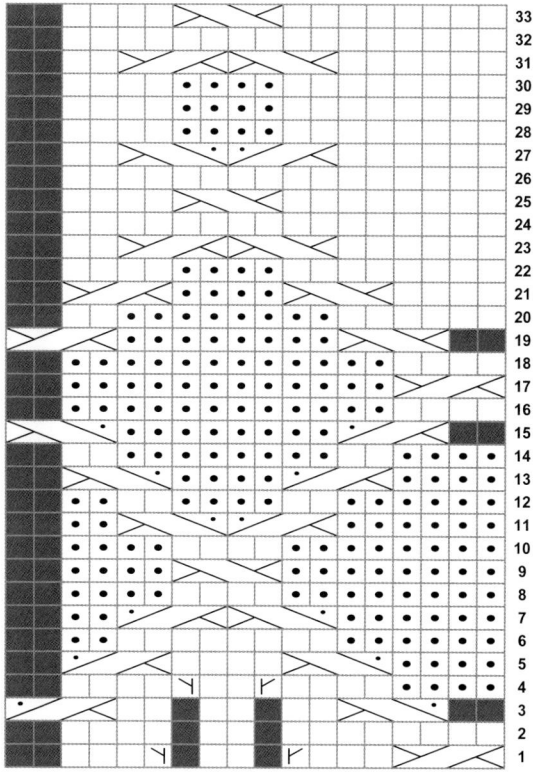

On Rnds 3, 15 & 19: Slip first 2 sts of rnd, rep chart across rnd, work final cable using last 2 sts of rnd and those 2 slipped sts, keeping BOR M in middle of cable.

LEGEND

■ **No Stitch** — Placeholder—no stitch made

☐ **Knit Stitch**

• **Purl Stitch**

M1R — Make 1 right-leaning stitch

M1L — Make 1 left-leaning stitch

2 over 2 Right Cable (2/2 RC) — Sl2 to CN, hold in back; K2, K2 from CN

2 over 2 Left Cable (2/2 LC) — Sl2 to CN, hold in front; K2, K2 from CN

2 over 2 Right Cable, Purl back (2/2 RPC) — Sl2 to CN, hold in back; K2, P2 from CN

2 over 2 Left Cable, Purl back (2/2 LPC) — Sl2 to CN, hold in front; P2, K2 from CN

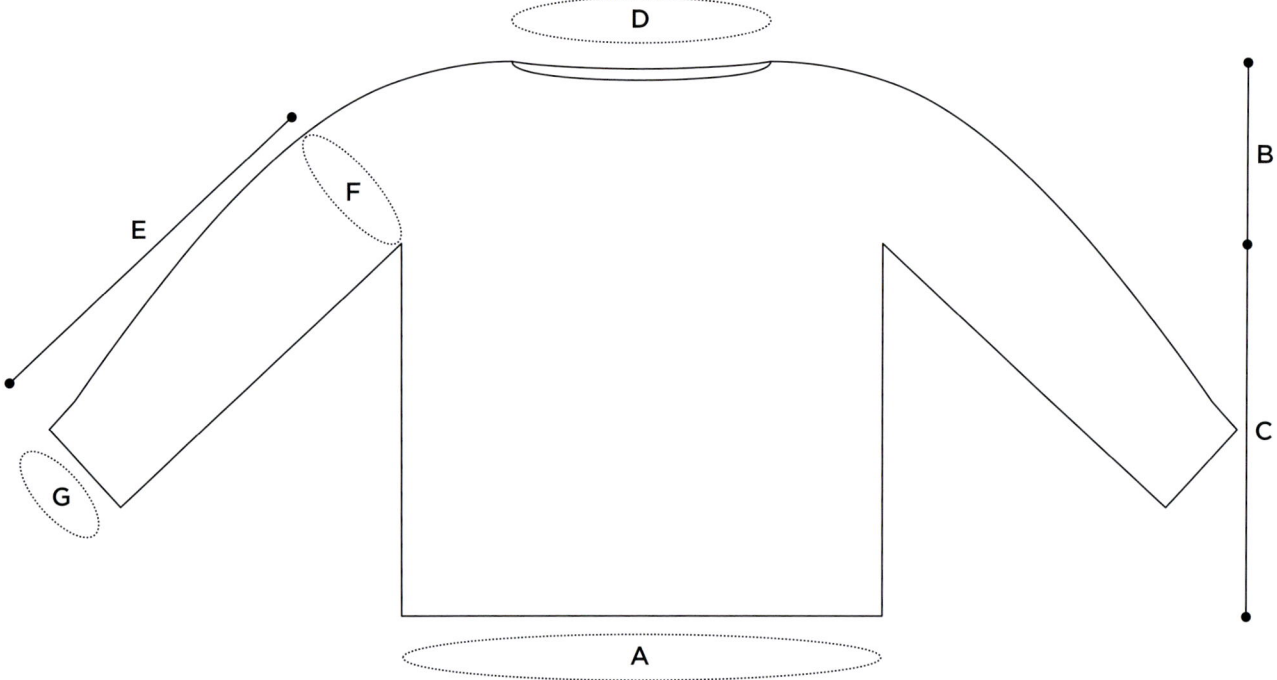

- **A** *chest circumference* 33 (37.25, 41, 45.25, 49)(53.25, 57.75, 61.25, 65.75)"
- **B** *yoke length* 8 (8, 8.25, 8.75, 9)(9.75, 10.25, 10.75, 11)"
- **C** *length to underarm* 17 (17, 18, 19, 19)(20, 20, 21, 21)"
- **D** *neck circumference* 23 (25.75, 26.75, 26.75, 26.75)(28.5, 27.5, 28.5, 28.5)"
- **E** *sleeve length* 19.5 (20, 20, 20.5, 20.5)(21, 21, 21, 21)"
- **F** *upper arm circumference* 12 (13.25, 14.25, 15.5, 16.5)(17.75, 19, 21, 22.25)"
- **G** *cuff circumference* 9.75 (9.75, 10.75, 10.75, 11.5)(11.5, 12.5, 13.25, 13.25)"

BALTER HAT
by Sierra Morningstar

FINISHED MEASUREMENTS

17.5 (21)" circumference × 9.75" height, with brim folded over (smaller size will stretch to accommodate an average adult head with a traditional, snug fit; if a looser, more relaxed fit is preferred, choose larger size)
Sample is 21"

YARN

Wool of the Andes™ Superwash (bulky weight, 100% Superwash Wool; 137 yards/100g): Mineral Heather 26514, 2 (2) hanks

NEEDLES

US 9 (5.5mm) 16" circular needles and DPNs, or size to obtain gauge

US 8 (5mm) 16" circular needles, or one size smaller than size used to obtain gauge

NOTIONS

Yarn Needle
Stitch Marker
Cable Needle
Jumbo Pom-Pom Maker (optional)

GAUGE

16 sts and 22 rnds = 4" in Reverse Stockinette Stitch in the round, blocked
20 sts and 23 rnds = 4" in 2x2 Rib, blocked but not stretched (note that this is approximate due to the amount of stretch in the ribbing)

For pattern support, contact Morn5420@yahoo.com

Balter Hat

Notes:

To balter is to dance, artlessly and without pretension, but with ample joy. This hat, covered with whimsical bobbles and circles, is the perfect companion for joyful frolics!

Balter features circular cables on top of a reverse stockinette stitch base. To create these cables, new stitches are created with a series of increases at the bottom, and then a single, 6-stitch decrease at the top.

Chart is worked in the round; read each chart row from right to left as a RS row.

3/1 LPC (3 over 1 Left Cable, Purl back)
Sl3 onto CN and hold in front; P1, K3 from CN.

3/1 RPC (3 over 1 Right Cable, Purl back)
Sl1 onto CN and hold in back; K3, P1 from CN.

3/2 LPC (3 over 2 Left Cable, Purl back)
Sl3 onto CN and hold in front; P2, K3 from CN.

3/2 RPC (3 over 2 Right Cable, Purl back)
Sl2 onto CN and hold in back; K3, P2 from CN.

3/3 LPC (3 over 3 Left Cable, Purl back)
Sl3 onto CN and hold in front; P3, K3 from CN.

3/3 RPC (3 over 3 Right Cable, Purl back)
Sl3 onto CN and hold in back; K3, P3 from CN.

MB (Make Bobble)
Step 1: K1, YO, K1, YO, K1 into next st. Turn work to back.
Step 2: P5. Turn work to front.
Step 3: K5. Turn work to back.
Step 4: P2tog, P1, P2tog. Turn work to front.
Step 5: SK2P. (1 st remains.)

CDI (Central Double Increase)
Knit into back of next st, then knit into front of same st, slipping this st off needle. With LH needle behind work, pick up strand of yarn that runs from st just worked across base of first st worked. Knit this st.

Dec7 (Decrease 7 to 1)
Step 1: Sl4 sts from LH needle to RH needle.
Step 2: Pass second st on RH needle over first st and off needle.
Step 3: Slip first st on RH needle back to LH needle. Pass second st on LH needle over first st and off needle.
Step 4: Slip first st on LH needle back to RH needle. Pass second st on RH needle over first st and off needle.
Rep Steps 3–4 one more time, then rep Step 3 once more. Purl next st on LH needle.

Circle Cable Pattern (in the rnd over a multiple of 14 sts)
Rnd 1: (MB, P13) to end.
Rnd 2: (P7, M1R, CDI, M1L, P6) to end. 90 (108) sts.
Rnd 3: *P7, K2 (K1, YO, K1) into the next st, K2, P6; rep from * to end. 100 (120) sts.
Rnd 4: (P4, 3/3 RPC, K1 TBL, 3/3 LPC, P3) to end.
Rnd 5: (P4, K3, P7, K3, P3) to end.
Rnd 6: (P2, 3/2 RPC, P7, 3/2 LPC, P1) to end.
Rnd 7: (P2, K3, P11, K3, P1) to end.
Rnd 8: (P1, 3/1 RPC, P11, 3/1 LPC) to end.
Rnds 9–12: (P1, K3, P13, K3) to end.
Rnd 13: (P1, 3/1 LPC, P11, 3/1 RPC) to end.
Rnd 14: (P2, K3, P11, K3, P1) to end.
Rnd 15: (P2, 3/2 LPC, P7, 3/2 RPC, P1) to end.
Rnd 16: (P4, K3, P7, K3, P3) to end.
Rnd 17: (P4, 3/3 LPC, P1, 3/3 RPC, P3) to end.
Rnd 18: (P7, Dec7, P6) to end. 70 (84) sts.
Rnd 19: Rep Rnd 1.

DIRECTIONS

Brim
With smaller circular needles and using Long Tail Cast On, or the method of your choice, CO 68 (76) sts. PM for BOR and join for working in the rnd, being careful not to twist sts. Work 2x2 Rib for 5".

Size 17.5" Inc Rnd: K17, M1, K34, M1, K17. 70 sts.

Size 21" Inc Rnd: K5, (M1, K9) two times, (M1, K10) three times, (M1, K9) two times, M1, K5. 84 sts.

Body (resume all sizes)
Change to larger needles.
Work Rev St st for six rnds.
Work Rnds 1–19 of Circle Cable Chart once, from chart or written instructions, repeating 5 (6) times around..
Work Rev St st for three rnds.

Crown
Change to DPNs when necessary.
Rnd 1: (P5, P2tog) to end. 60 (72) sts.
Rnd 2: P all.
Rnd 3: (P4, P2tog) to end. 50 (60) sts.
Rnd 4: P all.
Rnd 5: (P3, P2tog) to end. 40 (48) sts.
Rnd 6: P all.
Rnd 7: (P2, P2tog) to end. 30 (36) sts.
Rnd 8: P all.
Rnd 9: (P1, P2tog) to end. 20 (24) sts.
Rnd 10: P2tog 10 (12) times. 10 (12) sts.
Rnd 11: P2tog 5 (6) times. 5 (6) sts.

Finishing
Break yarn, leaving a long tail. With yarn needle, pull tail through remaining 5 (6) sts and pull tightly to close.
Weave in ends, wash, and block as desired.
Attach optional pom-pom as desired.

Circle Cable Pattern

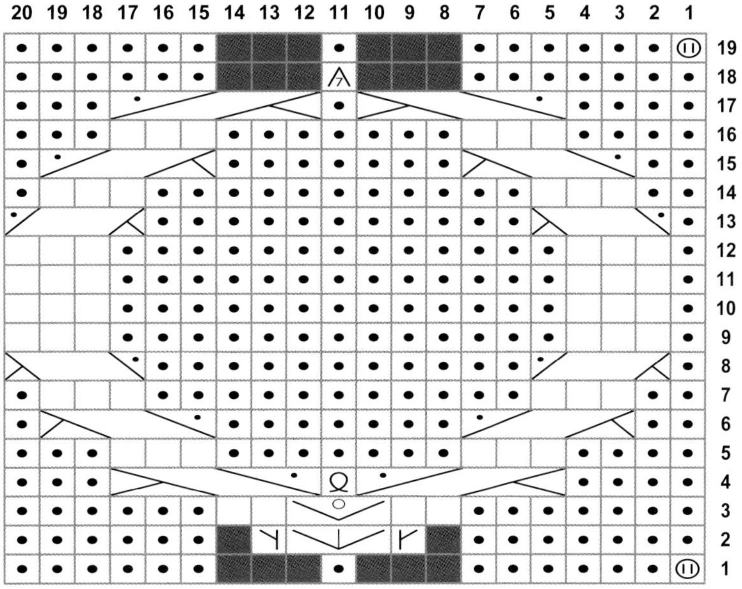

LEGEND

No Stitch
Placeholder—no stitch made

Knit Stitch

Purl Stitch

K TBL
Knit stitch through the back loop

Make Bobble (MB)
See *Notes* for instructions

M1R
Make 1 right-leaning stitch

M1L
Make 1 left-leaning stitch

Central Double Increase (CDI)
See *Notes* for instructions

K-YO-K
(Knit 1, Yarn Over, Knit 1) into 1 stitch

3 over 1 Right Cable, Purl back (3/1 RPC)
Sl1 to CN, hold in back; K3, P1 from CN

3 over 1 Left Cable, Purl back (3/1 LPC)
Sl3 to CN, hold in front; P1, K3 from CN

3 over 2 Right Cable, Purl back (3/2 RPC)
Sl2 to CN, hold in back; K3, P2 from CN

3 over 2 Left Cable, Purl back (3/2 LPC)
Sl3 to CN, hold in front; P2, K3 from CN

3 over 3 Right Cable, Purl back (3/3 RPC)
Sl3 to CN, hold in back; K3, P3 from CN

3 over 3 Left Cable, Purl back (3/3 LPC)
Sl3 to CN, hold in front; P3, K3 from CN

Decrease 7 to 1 (Dec7)
See *Notes*

Glossary
Common Stitches & Techniques

Slipped Stitches (Sl)
Always slip stitches purl-wise with yarn held to the wrong side of work, unless noted otherwise in the pattern.

Make 1 Left-Leaning Stitch (M1L)
Inserting LH needle from front to back, PU the horizontal strand between the st just worked and the next st, and K TBL.

Make 1 Right-Leaning Stitch (M1R)
Inserting LH needle from back to front, PU the horizontal strand between the st just worked and the next st, and K TFL.

Slip, Slip, Knit (SSK)
(Sl1 K-wise) twice; insert LH needle into front of these 2 sts and knit them together.

Centered Double Decrease (CDD)
Slip first and second sts together as if to work K2tog; K1; pass 2 slipped sts over the knit st.

Stockinette Stitch (St st, flat over any number of sts)
Row 1 (RS): Knit all sts.
Row 2 (WS): Purl all sts.
Rep Rows 1-2 for pattern.
St st in the round: Knit every rnd.
Rev St st is the opposite—purl on RS, knit on WS.

Garter Stitch (in the round over any number of sts)
Rnd 1: Purl all sts.
Rnd 2: Knit all sts.
Rep Rnds 1-2 for pattern.
Garter Stitch flat: Knit every row.
(One Garter *ridge* is comprised of two rows/rnds.)

1x1 Rib (flat or in the round, over an even number of sts)
Row/Rnd 1: (K1, P1) to end of row/rnd.
Rep Row/Rnd 1 for pattern.

2x2 Rib (flat over a multiple of 4 sts plus 2)
Row 1 (RS): K2, (P2, K2) to end of row.
Row 2 (WS): P2, (K2, P2) to end of row.
Rep Rows 1-2 for pattern.

2x2 Rib (in the round over a multiple of 4 sts)
Rnd 1: (K2, P2) to end of rnd.
Rep Rnd 1 for pattern.

Knitting in the Round
The Magic Loop technique uses one long circular needle to knit around a small circumference. The Two Circulars technique uses two long circular needles to knit around a small circumference. Photo and video tutorials for these, plus using DPNs and 16" circular needles, can be found at knitpicks.com/learning-center/knitting-in-round.

Backwards Loop Cast On
A simple, all-purpose cast on that can be worked mid-row. Also called Loop or Single Cast On. A tutorial can be found at knitpicks.com/learning-center/backwards-loop-cast-on.

Long Tail Cast On
Fast and neat once you get the hang of it. Also referred to as the Slingshot Cast On. A tutorial can be found at knitpicks.com/learning-center/learn-to-knit.

Cable Cast On
A strong and nice looking basic cast on that can be worked mid-project. A tutorial can be found at tutorials.knitpicks.com/cabled-cast-on.

Knitted Cast On
A basic cast on that can be worked mid-project. A tutorial can be found at knitpicks.com/learning-center/knitted-cast-on.

3-Needle Bind Off
Used to easily seam two rows of live stitches together. A tutorial can be found at knitpicks.com/learning-center/3-needle-bind-off.

Abbreviations

approx	approximately	KFB *(inc 1)*	knit into front and back of stitch	PSSO *(dec 1)*	pass slipped stitch over	SSP *(dec 1)*	slip, slip, purl these 2 stitches together through back loop
BO	bind off	K-wise	knit-wise	PU	pick up		
BOR	beginning of round	LH	left hand	P-wise	purl-wise	SSSK *(dec 2)*	slip, slip, slip, knit these 3 stitches together (like SSK)
CN	cable needle	M	marker	rep	repeat		
C (1, 2...)	color (1, 2...)	M1 *(inc 1)*	make 1 stitch (work same as M1L)	Rev St st	reverse stockinette stitch *(see above)*	St st	stockinette stitch *(see above)*
CC	contrast color						
CDD *(dec 2)*	centered double decrease *(see above)*	M1L *(inc 1)*	make 1 left-leaning stitch *(see above)*	RH	right hand	st(s)	stitch(es)
				rnd(s)	round(s)	TBL	through back loop
CO	cast on	M1R *(inc 1)*	make 1 right-leaning stitch *(see above)*	RS	right side	TFL	through front loop
cont	continue			Sk	skip	tog	together
dec(s)	decrease(es)			SK2P *(dec 2)*	slip K-wise, knit 2 together, pass slipped stitch over	W&T	wrap & turn *(see next page)*
DPN(s)	double pointed needle(s)	MC	main color				
		P	purl			WE	work even
inc(s)	increase(s)	P2tog *(dec 1)*	purl 2 stitches together	SKP *(dec 1)*	slip K-wise, knit, pass slipped stitch over	WS	wrong side
K	knit					WYIB	with yarn in back
K2tog *(dec 1)*	knit 2 stitches together	P3tog *(dec 2)*	purl 3 stitches together	Sl	slip *(see above)*	WYIF	with yarn in front
				SM	slip marker		
K3tog *(dec 2)*	knit 3 stitches together	PM	place marker	SSK *(dec 1)*	slip, slip, knit these 2 stitches together *(see above)*	YO *(inc 1)*	bring yarn over needle from front up over to back
		PFB *(inc 1)*	purl into front and back of stitch				

Cables
Tutorials for different kinds of cables, including 1 over 1 and 2 over 2, with and without cable needles, can be found at knitpicks.com/learning-center/guides/cables.

Felted Join (to splice yarn)
One method for joining a new length of yarn to the end of one that is already being used. A tutorial can be found at tutorials.knitpicks.com/felted-join.

Mattress Stitch
A neat, invisible seaming method that uses the bars between the first and second stitches on the edges. A tutorial can be found at tutorials.knitpicks.com/mattress-stitch.

Provisional Cast On (crochet method)
Used to cast on stitches that are also a row of live stitches, so they can be put onto a needle and used later.
DIRECTIONS: Using a crochet hook, make a slip knot, then hold knitting needle in left hand, hook in right. With yarn in back of needle, work a chain st by pulling yarn over needle and through chain st. Move yarn back to behind needle, and rep for the number of sts required. Chain a few more sts off the needle, then break yarn and pull end through last chain. (CO sts may be incorrectly mounted; if so, work into backs of these sts.) To unravel later (when sts need to be picked up), pull chain end out; chain should unravel, leaving live sts. A video tutorial can be found at tutorials.knitpicks.com/crocheted-provisional-cast-on.

Provisional Cast On (crochet chain method)
Same result as the crochet method above, but worked differently, so you may prefer one or the other.
DIRECTIONS: With a crochet hook, use scrap yarn to make a slip knot and chain the number of sts to be cast on, plus a few extra sts. Insert tip of knitting needle into first bump of crochet chain. Wrap project yarn around needle as if to knit, and pull yarn through crochet chain, forming first st. Rep this process until you have cast on the correct number of sts. To unravel later (when sts need to be picked up), pull chain out, leaving live sts. A photo tutorial can be found at tutorials.knitpicks.com/crocheted-provisional-cast-on.

Judy's Magic Cast On
This method creates stitches coming out in opposite directions from a seamless center line, perfect for starting toe-up socks.
DIRECTIONS: Make a slip knot and place loop around one of the two needles; anchor loop counts as first st. Hold needles tog, with needle that yarn is attached to on top. In other hand, hold yarn so tail goes over index finger and yarn attached to ball goes over thumb. Bring tip of bottom needle over strand of yarn on finger (top strand), around and under yarn and back up, making a loop around needle. Pull loop snug. Bring top needle (with slip knot) over yarn tail on thumb (bottom strand), around and under yarn and back up, making a loop around needle. Pull loop snug. Cont casting on sts until desired number is reached; top yarn strand always wraps around bottom needle, and bottom yarn strand always wraps around top needle. A tutorial can be found at tutorials.knitpicks.com/judys-magic-cast-on.

Stretchy Bind Off
DIRECTIONS: K2, *insert LH needle into front of 2 sts on RH needle and knit them tog—1 st remains on RH needle. K1; rep from * until all sts have been bound off. A tutorial can be found at tutorials.knitpicks.com/go-your-own-way-socks-toe-up-part-7-binding-off.

Jeny's Surprisingly Stretchy Bind Off (for 1x1 Rib)
DIRECTIONS: Reverse YO, K1, pass YO over; *YO, P1, pass YO and previous st over P1; reverse YO, K1, pass YO and previous st over K1; rep from * until 1 st is left, then break working yarn and pull it through final st to complete BO.

Kitchener Stitch (also called Grafting)
Seamlessly join two sets of live stitches together.
DIRECTIONS: With an equal number of sts on two needles, break yarn leaving a tail approx four times as long as the row of sts, and thread through a blunt yarn needle. Hold needles parallel with WSs facing in and both needles pointing to the right. Perform Step 2 on the first front st, then Step 4 on the first back st, then continue from Step 1, always pulling yarn tightly so the grafted row tension matches the knitted fabric:
Step 1: Pull yarn needle K-wise through front st and drop st from knitting needle.
Step 2: Pull yarn needle P-wise through next front st, leaving st on knitting needle.
Step 3: Pull yarn needle P-wise through first back st and drop st from knitting needle.
Step 4: Pull yarn needle K-wise through next back st, leaving st on knitting needle.
Rep Steps 1–4 until all sts have been grafted together, finishing by working Step 1 through the last remaining front st, then Step 3 through the last remaining back st. Photo tutorials can be found at knitpicks.com/learning-center/learn-to-knit/kitchener.

Short Rows
There are several options for how to handle short rows, so you may see different suggestions/instructions in a pattern.

Wrap and Turn (W&T) (one option for Short Rows)
Work until the st to be wrapped. If knitting: Bring yarn to front, Sl next st P-wise, return yarn to back; turn work, and Sl wrapped st onto RH needle. Cont across row. If purling: Bring yarn to back of work, Sl next st P-wise, return yarn to front; turn work and Sl wrapped st onto RH needle. Cont across row. **Picking up Wraps:** Work to wrapped st. If knitting: Insert RH needle under wrap, then through wrapped st K-wise; K st and wrap tog. If purling: Sl wrapped st P-wise onto RH needle, use LH needle to lift wrap and place it onto RH needle; Sl wrap and st back onto LH needle, and P tog. A tutorial for W&T can be found at tutorials.knitpicks.com/short-rows-wrap-and-turn-or-wt.

German Short Rows (another option for Short Rows)
Work to turning point; turn. WYIF, Sl first st P-wise. Bring yarn over back of right needle, pulling firmly to create a "double stitch" on RH needle. If next st is a K st, leave yarn at back; if next st is a P st, bring yarn to front between needles. When it's time to work into double st, knit both strands tog. A video tutorial for German Short Rows can be found at knitpicks.com/video/german-short-rows.

THIS COLLECTION FEATURES

Capra™
DK Weight
85% Fine Merino Wool, 15% Cashmere

City Tweed™
Aran Weight
55% Merino Wool, 25% Superfine Alpaca, 20% Donegal Tweed

Gloss™
Fingering & DK Weights
70% Merino Wool, 30% Silk

High Desert™
Sport & Worsted Weights
100% American Wool

Swish™
DK & Worsted Weights
100% Fine Superwash Merino Wool

Twill™
Worsted Weight
100% Superwash Merino Wool

Wool of the Andes™
Sport & Worsted Weights
100% Peruvian Highland Wool

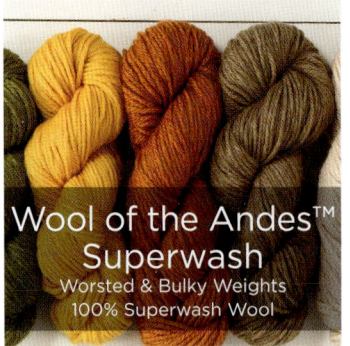

Wool of the Andes™ Superwash
Worsted & Bulky Weights
100% Superwash Wool

View these beautiful yarns and more at www.KnitPicks.com

Knit Picks yarn is both luxe and affordable—a seeming contradiction trounced! But it's not just about the pretty colors; we also care deeply about fiber quality and fair labor practices, leaving you with a gorgeously reliable product you'll turn to time and time again.